I Speak For
The Dead

By Joye M.
Carter, M.D.

Biblical Dogs™

I Speak for the Dead

Publisher's Cataloging-in-Publication
(Provided by Quality Books, Inc.)

Carter, Joye M., 1957-
    I speak for the dead / by Joye M. Carter. -- 1st ed.
    p. cm.
    LCCN 2002091650
    ISBN 0-9703722-3-X

    1. Death.   1. Title.

HQ1073./C37 2002   306.9
                      QB102-200627

Printed in the United States of America
Printed on acid free paper

Biblical Dogs™

Jacket design by Dreu Pennington-McNeil

Jacket photograph by Andre Santos

Dedication

This book is dedicated to my family and friends and the creator of mankind,

In memory of Reverend Tonya L. Fields and Reverend Richard S. Fitch,

To all of those in the midst of healing,

And lastly, to my beloved Sampson.

Acknowledgements

This book would never have been brought to fruition if it had not been for the talent of a few individuals like the ones mentioned below:

To Carol Renee Burnet for her patient transcription and having to read my left-handed writing.

To Andre Santos for his wonderful photography.

To Judy Robertson for her full-time assistance and watchful eyes.

To Chandra Sparks-Taylor for her brilliant editing which pulled more from me than I was willing to give at times.

To my Godparents, Pat and Charlie Smith, for always inspiring me.

To my pastor, Reverend Lawson, for his kindness.

To Sara and Mack for their guidance.

To Mom for her encouragement and to my sister, Sharon, for always providing a place to lay my head.

To my friends who kept me flowing and allowed me to be absent.

To Clifford for his down-to-earth opinions and who helped me find Drew with her wonderful artistry.

To all the people who asked for this work.

And, with pride, to my ancestors!

◆

Contents

Preface

"This is a critical and timely book. As many volumes as are churned out by motivational writers for the income, none have the breadth of insight and the depth of wisdom of *I Speak for the Dead*. As a leading medical examiner, Dr. Carter has a perspective that is both realistic and gentle, and is a natural outgrowth, not only of her professional experience but also of her personal faith in God. All adults should read it, whether or not you anticipate the death of a loved one or acquaintance in the future."

Reverend William A. Lawson

Wheeler Avenue Baptist Church

Houston, Texas

9

Foreword

"As a colleague, neighbor and friend, I have had the fortune and pleasure of knowing Dr. Joye Carter for many years. I have observed her commitment to her medical profession and to the people she has served, both alive and dead. She has never allowed external pressures to interfere with her compassion, her deliverance of medical service, or her easy manner in dealing with touchy subjects such as death.

In this, her second book, Dr. Carter has again demonstrated her understanding of the conflicting feelings and thoughts that surviving families and friends feel when death comes, whether expectedly or unexpectedly. The fear, relief, guilt, and peace create confusion and anger. The mixture of emotions sunprises even the more mature and experienced

11

people. Many times, they feel uninformed and isolated. This can lead the grievers to seek solace and healing in unhealthy ways.

Dr. Carter provides great insight into the subject of death. It is a subject many of us would like to ignore but all of us will eventually experience during our lifetime and at the end of this life.

Dr. Carter realized what many doctors fail to grasp throughout their professional lives, that death is not always the worst option. Her solid, unshakeable faith has given her the courage to not only deal with death on a routine basis, but to actually stop and examine this process of life without fear or resentment. Her philosophy is, 'not to fear death, but to learn from it'. Her personal stories in this book are instructional and inspirational.

In addition, Dr. Carter has practical advice on how to live our lives to the fullest while being fully aware of death as an inevitable process. She shows us that although we should be aware that when we die, we may be moving to another level of existence where the small worries of this world are not important, we should also be aware that we may leave behind our loved ones who must deal with the "messes" we leave behind for them to clean up. We will be able to help give the survivors some peace of mind, if we have taken care of affairs during our lifetime.

In this great reading, Dr. Carter has shown that her positive outlook about death and life has made her strong so that she can help support and guide us in our loving and mourning. And, as a survivor of the death of a loved one, Dr. Carter gives some suggestions of ways to mourn and then heal from the loss of a relationship.

Thankfully, there are those like Dr. Carter who secure dignity for the dying patient when that person may have lost almost everything else, who bring solace to families having difficulty making decisions for the terminally ill and difficulty in letting go, who secure dignity for the physicians who make medical decisions, and who examine the bodies of the deceased to provide answers to questions of families and friends, resolve conflicts and, hopefully, give peace to all.

We can learn from the advice, stories and words of wisdom that Dr. Carter gives to us in this book."

Edith Irby Jones, M.D.
Houston, Texas

14

ECCLESIASTES 3:1-8

To every thing there is a season; and a time to every purpose under the heaven:

A time to be born, and a time to die; a time to plant, and a time to pluck up that which is planted;

A time to kill, a time to heal; a time to break down, and a time to build up;

A time to weep, and a time to laugh, a time to mourn, and a time to dance;

A time to cast away stones, and a time to gather stones together; a time to embrace, and a time to refrain from embracing;

A time to get, and a time to lose; a time to keep, and a time to cast away;

A time to rend, and a time to sew; a time to keep silent, and a time to speak;

A time to love, and a time to hate; a time of war, and a time of peace.

15

Introduction

What do the following phases have in common? These phrases may sound familiar to some and mysterious to others. He caught the train, went to Chicago, went to meet his maker, went home, he is out of here, went South, kicked the bucket, home going, gone to his father's place, had the O sign, bit the dust, crossed over, showed the Q sign, or he was lost. They are all ways to say that somebody has died without using the word death. More than anything the use of these terms sums up the uncomfortable feeling that most people have about the topic of death. It is the great unknown. It remains a great mystery and it is human nature, I suppose, to fear, what we cannot understand. Frankly, people have never been able to understand why we have to die. I do not have the answer to that question and I certainly know that we cannot predict, for the most part, when anyone will die. The bible teaches us three score plus ten for a lifespan. It has been popular in recent years for people to say that they have been close to death and have described experiencing a white light and a sense of comfort at that time, but there has not been a documented study or thesis to clarify exactly what death is. "Death happens," as some people say. We have all heard, "Life is short, use every day wisely." I believe very much in this latter phrase, but the fact remains that when we begin to talk about death, people become uncomfortable.

When I am asked what I do for a living and I respond that death investigation is my chosen specialty, a hush falls over the room. I am usually asked in an incredulous tone, "You mean you work with dead people?" I reply, "Absolutely," with no hesitation. The next question is, "How can you do that?" My answer is just as rapid, " I believe in God."

I believe in the resurrection of Christ. I believe with all my heart that the essence of humanity is not just the physical body. It is a spirit, a soul, an intellect, and a personality. It is whatever you call it or know it to be. I consider life to be energy. When death occurs, that energy or spirit leaves the body and what we have left are the human remains. Based upon my religious beliefs, I have never had any need to fear the dead. I have never been reluctant to use the word death but I realize that it cannot be used in every situation, largely because so many people fear the concept. As a practical matter, it has always been my belief that people who have died are no longer in pain. They cannot be hurt anymore. Their soul has gone to another dimension. I have always believed that peace is found in death. In my line of work, the best thing that I can do at the time of death is to perform the most thorough examination on the human remains that I possibly can. It becomes my responsibility as a forensic pathologist and death investigator to document what has happened to the deceased; not to fear death, but to learn from it.

Shakespeare once wrote in *Romeo and Juliet*, "A rose by any other name would smell as sweet." Likewise, no matter what we call it, death will occur. You can only change the term so much. The implication is the same. In my book, death is the great equalizer. No matter who we are, what our station is in life, what advantages or disadvantages we have had as people, death occurs in all populations, all socioeconomic levels, all neighborhoods, and to all skin colors.

I feel that as a physician I must be honest with families who are counting on me for information. I try to use realistic terms that are soft, but also convey information about what happened to their loved one.

This book is an attempt to fill a void in medical and nonfiction literature. When death causes an individual we know and love to forever be separated from us, we as survivors need to be cared for. We need to be talked to. We need to understand. I believe that survivors have questions that often go unanswered when death separates a relationship.

Please accept this work as information and insight from one who deals with the dead.

God bless those who are left behind.

Joye M. Carter, M.D.

I Accept My Gift

At the tender age of fourteen, I made two of the most important decisions of my life. One was to reconfirm my belief in God. The second was to accept the introduction to a forensic pathology career as it had been presented to me. Many adults assume that young people cannot possibly be serious about a career choice at such a young age, but I was. I was committed to working in my church, striving to live a life as a Christian teenager. It was not easy being confronted with all the complexities of life and trying to manage being a good person, a scholar, and navigate through the difficult decisions of my young adult years. I was fortunate to have a wonderful church home and supportive family and godparents.

You learn quickly as a young adult that when you are not doing what everyone else does it can be difficult, if not disastrous, for your self-esteem. Be that as it may, I continued to work toward both goals because I believed that there was something greater in store for me.

Some thirty years later I know that I could not have succeeded in becoming a physician, particularly a forensic pathologist, if it had not been for my strong belief in God, in the Bible, or in the biblical descriptions of heaven and hell. It is important that I publicly state that my desire, curiosity, and progression in this career choice is a recognizable gift bestowed on me earlier in my life and one that has led me places that I never imagined.

Looking back, my lack of fear could only be attributed to the fact that I have believed that death is a beginning of a new phase of existence. Not everyone can do what I can do, nor should they try.

I think we all have certain assigned tasks. I was fortunate to recognize mine when I did. Although, I always wanted to be a doctor, I could never stand to watch a person suffer. By the same token I was never fond of all the drugs that patients tend to be prescribed in this country.

While working as a volunteer in emergency rooms I recall feeling such empathy for patients in pain. I knew that patient care was not going to be my chosen field of medicine. I always wondered what I could do to help somebody who was in agony. What could I do to make someone comfortable? Those questions were never answered for me in the clinical studies of medicine. I always felt a sense of being powerless in dealing with the injured. Yet, when it came to the gentle handling of the dead, I realized I was in my element. Unusual, some would say, but for me a natural gift.

My ability to deal with the human body is a much treasured skill, as is my ability to retain deep sensitivity and the knowledge that all people's needs and emotional losses have to be considered when their loved one dies. I am so grateful to God for allowing me to retain this sense in a career where it is so easy to become jaded. I know that the family, friends, or people affected by a traumatic loss need to be treated the same way that I would want my family treated if something happened to me.

Since death is the great equalizer, it should not make a difference what the dead person's ethnic background was, nor should it make a difference if he had a college degree or if the person had a home. What matters most is that we are all human beings. We all share this world and, in fact, all of us will have our own time to die.

The topic of death is hardly ever good dinner conversation. In using my gift, I want to bring about a greater understanding of the death investigation process, the changes that occur at death, and attempt to convey the information that is learned from examining a dead body. The main reason to do this is for the survivors' sake. I want to help family and friends to understand and handle the fact that their loved one has died. There is no such thing as, "You will get over it." When you love somebody, you never get over that person's death. The pain may lessen with time, but you never forget the person. There will always be a void, which may become narrow as time marches on but will never be completely filled. I want to reassure the bereaved family and friends that they will have their own way and rhythm of adjustment. Recovering from the grief of death often depends on the intensity of the intimate relationship between the grieving survivor and the individual who has died.

Sometimes we in the health field are seen as callous because we are removed from the intimate interaction between two human beings. Sometimes health professionals become embarrassed when death occurs, particularly a personal physician. Our doctors are at a loss because they feel their professional inadequacies have allowed death to occur. We, as health-care professionals and scientists, are taught that we avenge and fight off death, but it is rarely emphasized that sometimes we lose the battle. It is important to remember that we battle the unknown, the unseen, and the unpredictable. It is equally important to remember that despite all of our efforts, all of our collective medical knowledge, and despite the loved ones' wishes, death will occur.

My gift is the comfortable way in which I can discuss death and the many aspects that are associated with the dying process. I hope, by sharing this information, I am able to convey the message that death is part of a cycle of life, and we cannot always prepare for it.

Oftentimes, we who are left behind must simply deal with our loss until such time that we are in control of our grief and have come to accept the absence of our loved one. The topics covered in this book will seem sad, depressing, horrifying, or just plain distasteful to some. To those individuals, I urge you to continue to read so that you might understand. To others who are hurting and seeking comfort, I hope that you find some closure in a way that will help you to recognize that you are not alone in your struggle to handle the death of a loved one.

When I state that I speak for the dead, I truly mean these words. I feel that as a forensic pathologist and physician, it is my duty to care for the deceased. I did not know the person as a patient and I cannot communicate verbally with him. My responsibility is to thoroughly document the death. My gift is to learn from that examination, take the information back to the living, to help them understand why death occurred and to help others live longer, safer, and healthier lives. If I fail to pass on this information, if I fail to lend respect to that dead person, if I fail to treat the deceased as I would treat my loved ones, then I am wasting my gift.

As a person of great religious faith I must accept the responsibilities that accompany my talent. That means using a gift for the purpose that it was intended. When you are of great religious faith and you take an oath, you accept the responsibility that comes with it. I took the oath of Hippocrates. Every graduating medical student in this country takes it. In layman's terms the oath says, "First, do no harm." When you absorb the strength of words of the Hippocratic oath you will understand why so many physicians devote their lives to their practices and to the well being of patients. As you read this book I hope that you can embrace the power of these words and that whatever your gift has been revealed to be, or will be in the future, that you accept the responsibility of that talent. If you do not use your gifts for the good of mankind, then they are wasted.

Denial, The Problem

Because we as human beings, for the most part, do not want to face the prospect of our own demise, we avoid the subject. It is unpleasant and difficult to contemplate your own death. We often feel that nothing will happen to us, only to the other guy. Unfortunately, too many people have had this thought. We cannot afford to be in denial all of our lives.

How many people carry credit cards, a driver's license, money, or business cards in their wallet? I bet quite a few. How many have a phone number or address for someone who should be contacted if something happens? Most people are reluctant to fill out those *In-Case-of-Emergency* cards. It is a symptom of denial. The topic of identification is a sensitive one, and one rarely thought about until an emergency. Most of us go about our daily activities without thinking about who we are. That is for someone else to think about when the time comes. Many people go out to parties, exercising, or visiting without any identification. Why? Because we don't believe anything will ever happen to us. This is not peculiar to any one age group. It is human nature to believe that we will always be safe and sound and always return home. I am here to tell you that safe arrival does not happen all the time!

One of the worst things to contemplate is that your loved one may have been seriously injured or killed. If that happens, however, you would like to know what happened. Approximately thirty percent of all the bodies that are examined in the medical examiner's office in Houston, Texas, come in as unidentified for nearly twenty-four hours. The rationale is that most of these individuals had no identification on their person at the time of their demise. There are delays in notifying next-of-kin when tragedy strikes because there is no easy way to find out who the deceased person was or how to locate their family.

Freak accidents will happen in the workplace, on public transportation, or even on the sidewalk. There have been numerous occasions in my experience where people have even died in churches, at weddings, or even at a loved one's funeral.

We often overlook opportunities where we can discuss a means of verifying identification with our loved ones, those we care about, or those for whom we are responsible. I believe that every person should have an identification card that somehow links him to his surroundings, his family, his friends, an organization, or to someone who can say that he was known to a particular community. In our fast-paced world, with so much transcontinental mobility, there are individuals who, unfortunately, have met their demise while traveling for business or pleasure, and it takes quite a while to notify the loved ones. If for no other reason than for clarity of mind, keep identification on your body or in your wallet.

Denial is broad when it comes to considering the occurrence of death. One such area of concern that I witness all too regularly is the condition of our senior citizens. We miss the opportunity to discuss with our elders what they may want to have done should they become unable to make decisions about their care or in the event of their death. Many times while counseling families, there is so much grief and guilt because the family, particularly the adult children, have had to make a decision that they were not sure that their parent or loved one would have wanted made. There are a lot of questions that go along with the guilt. *What would my loved one have wanted?*

Sometimes a situation involves making decisions about extensive medical or surgical intervention, prolonging life mechanically, or just deciding whether or not a person would want to have a blood transfusion. It takes so much emotional energy for loved ones to make these decisions when it has never been discussed with the person beforehand. Once your loved one has lost the ability to communicate or if he becomes unconscious or suffers a traumatic injury and is not expected to survive, it can be all the more painful to make that decision.

We all, at some point, should sit down with our family and have that conversation about end-of-life care. If you live by yourself, make up your mind and share that decision with your doctor, minister, or a friend if you do not have significant others to tell. It is difficult to approach this topic because it is frightening when you think about the loss of someone whose company you are used to. My advice is to start the conversation off by saying, "We need to talk. I love you. I do not want to frighten you, but I just want to know, in case a decision should become necessary for you to make, this is what I would like to have done." Once you have that conversation, there will be some comfort in knowing that you have expressed your wishes.

There is another area where denial plays a role and it is always a bitter pill to swallow. That is the notion that we may live forever and will have time to retract harsh words or make up for bad behavior. It is so sad when an individual dies suddenly and he has been in a verbal altercation with a loved one. There is no way to take back words when you are not sure if the person hears you anymore. The grief, the anxiety, and the trauma are almost unimaginable. I sometimes wonder what people would say if they were arguing and in the middle of that argument they thought, *Would I continue this line of conversation if I knew I would never see this person again and could never hold him or look into his eyes?*

My personal philosophy has been to not go to bed angry, to consider the worst-case scenario, and to appreciate those I have in my life. So many times, family members will come to the morgue to identify their loved one's body and they are racked with physical pain and emotional anguish, crying because they never had the chance to say, "I'm sorry." We never know if we will get the chance to say we are sorry. The additional stress that a survivor suffers when the death of a friend occurs during an unresolved argument often delays their grief reaction. The grieving process becomes prolonged as the person sorts out his feelings.

Another unfortunate incident occurs when there has not been communication in a family or in a relationship and it focuses on what to do with the deceased individual's body. The worst confrontations have been witnessed at hospitals, at the morgue, or even during the funeral when there is discord between family members. I have witnessed disgruntled extended families fighting over what to do with a body. The decedent becomes a tug-of-war. Most of the time, the emotions are not necessarily anger toward one another, but due to the loss of not having said good-bye to the deceased. Sometimes regrets and resentment by the parents about an adult child extends from a poor relationship with the son or daughter and is only revealed upon a person's death. Many times these battles become public, and ultimately disrespectful of the loved one's memory.

Sometimes individuals die without leaving wills or legally ending relationships. Often the next of kin's designation becomes a matter for a court to decide. It is not unusual to have someone die and his body come to the medical examiner's office where it is discovered there was more than one girlfriend or boyfriend or sometimes more than one spouse, and oftentimes the parties did not know the other existed. Children may find out when it is too late that a parent has died because they were never told the decedent was a relative. All these situations, in and of themselves, are sad, but many of them could have been avoided if conversation had just taken place.

How much time would it take to sit down, write out your desires about medical care, funeral plans, or a will? Probably not much. It would be so helpful to set priorities, to have dealt with an attorney, your doctor, or your confidante so that somebody would know your wishes and implement them in a timely manner. It would relieve the decision maker from the guilt of wondering, *Am I doing the right thing?* I know it is difficult to consider these issues when someone is standing right in front of you, full of life and love, with hopes for a bright future, but when these decisions are made, discussed, and agreed upon, there will be relief. When the time comes, the appropriate decisions have already been made.

The suggestion, and my point here, is that communication would solve many problems in a time of grief. I urge you to consult with your personal attorney, physician, religious leader, spouse, or friend to consider any kind of advance directives that will allow a person to make decisions about your healthcare should you be unable to do so. Share your thoughts on burial programs, legal wills, and Last Will and Testaments. We tend to put these important decisions off. Some people feel that they have nothing to leave their loved ones, and therefore, do not pursue any legal assistance. Some people feel that it is too expensive. If you give consideration to those for whom you are responsible, you will find a way to address some of these issues. All that I can say is that I have seen the intense pain that rests upon the shoulders of the surviving loved ones when this decision making has not been done. We cannot afford to live in denial.

Tomorrow is not promised.

Why We Hesitate To Donate

When death happens to someone we know, issues that we have not discussed with our loved ones such as looking at division of assets, filling out insurance papers, or asking a friend to take care of your children in the event of your untimely death become important. These are all difficult situations to consider. The general fear is that if we think about these situations or if we do the legal work then death will come quicker.

One particular area that comes to mind is the reason people don't fill out an organ/tissue donor card. When I speak of donor cards I mean that access by which organizations can remove life-saving organs or tissue from your body after death. Technology has changed and progressed so much in the last twenty years. Many adults and children who would have died a couple of decades ago from disease or from congenital anomalies are now able to live through the grace and kindness of people who donate parts of their body or their loved ones' bodies for organ and tissue procurement. The questionable issue that comes up at the time of death is what the deceased person would have wanted to be done with his body.

Currently, because it is such an emotional and ethical issue, the surviving loved ones have the right to say "yes" or "no" to tissue and organs being removed from the deceased. The problem is that many times family members do not know what the deceased would have wanted. That means, the opportunity to give a life-saving organ might be missed because of the length of time that it takes for someone to make a decision. It is now federal law that a person being admitted to a hospital or health-care facility must be asked, if he is over the age of eighteen, whether he would like to donate their organs. A death at a hospital must also be reported first to the organ procurement agency in that region so that representatives can approach the family and ask if they would like to donate the organs or tissues of the recently deceased.

I have questioned more than five hundred people who have not considered or made a decision about organ donation. Their main reason is that they were afraid to deal with the issue of their impending death. This kind of fear leaves a tremendous burden on their family because family members will not have any clue about their relatives' wishes and they will probably not be comfortable with the issue.

From a personal perspective, I made a decision many years ago that if part of my body was intact, in good condition, and available then I would like to have it donated to save a life. I think that it is the right thing to do. I know that most religious orders believe that this is the right thing to do and they encourage that sharing aspect. There is tremendous need in all communities and all ethnic backgrounds. I also know that transplantation works. I know these techniques have the ability to be done properly, ethically, and morally. I do what I can to educate the public to be aware of the procedures that are being performed and to make a decision early. A decision does not mean anything unless you share it with somebody, so again I encourage individuals to share their decision with their family, physician, attorney, or religious leader.

You must discuss your decision with your family. Organ donation is a traumatic question for the survivors to consider, and it is an especially difficult time if there is an unexpected loss.

The fear people have that they are going to die or be allowed to die prevents many from donating organs and tissue. The complete autopsy procedure ensures the recipient of the organs and tissues that there was no evidence of tumor, infection, or other diseases. The medical examiner or forensic pathologist acts as a gateway. We make sure that the records are reviewed; that the individual who was being treated for an illness or injury was given the best of care and that nothing is wrong in the health-care records.

Fear that emergency medical personnel will not attempt everything possible to save lives causes many to be resistant to signing a donor card. Part of this fear is based upon the unequal access to healthcare that many poor and minority populations deal with on a daily basis. One of the reasons that there are required divisions between the healthcare team and the organ procurement team is to relieve

this suspicion of premature deaths. There are

checks and balances in this system. As the medical

examiner, I represent one of them. I review all the

hospital records and the emergency-care records to

satisfy my responsibility that proper procedures

were utilized in caring for a patient.

Another reason why people are not willing

to document their ability to be an organ or tissue

donor is because they feel the system takes

advantage of individuals who do not have medical

or legal knowledge. I am addressing the issue of

presumed consent laws that exist in at least twenty-

five states that deal with the right of organ/tissue

procurement agencies to remove certain tissues

from a body without gaining informed consent from

the family. Most of these laws apply to the corneal

tissue, the clear part over the iris or the colored

portion of the eyes. This, of course, can be removed without disfiguring the decedent's face and without entering the body cavity. Rarely does it disfigure the body or interfere with the death investigation. What becomes important, of course, is the issue that there is no need to obtain consent. In fact, the way most of the laws are written, if the medical examiner or coroner knows of no objection by the family, then the corneal tissue may be removed at his or her direction.

These laws were not written by medical examiners. They were written by tissue procurement organizations. Presumed consent laws often puts a medical examiner in the uncomfortable position of not knowing what a family would have wanted if the family had known the law existed. Forensic pathologists, as well as organ procurement agencies know that most people do not realize that these presumed consent laws exist, so how can they

protest? How can you deny something being done

if you do not know that it is being done? That is

what I find unacceptable about these types of laws.

They were passed at the state legislative level

without an appropriate amount of public awareness.

The only way to make the system fair is to do

continuous public education.

In order for me not to compromise my ethics

in organ and tissue procurement, I prefer to educate

the public on a continuous basis. I feel that as a

medical examiner I have the responsibility of

working with everybody, and I mean everybody. I

encourage the tissue banks to make their procedures

known because they are being applied in the office

in which I currently work. Texas has some of the

oldest presumed consent laws, and every now and

then a family is quite disturbed to find that the

corneal tissue was removed from their loved one's body without their consent or knowledge. Wherever I go to speak on organ and tissue donation or presumed consent, I ask that people attending the meeting or conference go back to their home states and check the laws. This could affect any one of your loved ones or a family member who is traveling out of state or attending school out of state. If the corneas could not be taken in your home state, they could possibly be taken in another area. Proper donation is always a matter of public education. I do not believe that these laws are fair because they take advantage of individuals who do not have a lot of education or medical knowledge.

On the other hand, it is a constant education process to make tissue banks aware that they need to be culturally sensitive. This, in particular, applies to the African-American and Hispanic communities. Many of these organ procurement and tissue groups have hired what I call, "Cultural liaisons." In other words, these are employees who have rapport with individuals in their particular ethnic communities whom they can approach to ask if they would consider the option of donation. While I believe it is good to have a person who is culturally sensitive to groups' questions or concerns, I think it is somewhat unfair to have these individuals interact with only certain segments of the population. Within the organ procurement organizations, these cultural or community liaison employees hardly ever move up the ladder in terms of authority within the transplant organization. Most of the complaints that I have received from citizens are that the ads are insensitive to the poor and to the people of color. Other complaints center on the question of whether or not the public ads are

purposefully misleading in order to raise the
number of donors in a particular subset of the
community. The lack of diversity in the upper
management of the organ and tissue procurement
agencies is reflected in the style and composition of
some of their public ad campaigns.

Today, when you examine the
organizational structure of the agencies that procure
tissues and organs, there are only a few minorities
who have been able to move into the ranks of
management, or to the level of the advisory board
that governs the activities of the organ procurement
agencies. These groups should be honest. Do not
just hire a person to approach someone else. Hire
them to work with the community and to represent
all levels of the organization. If the liaison people
did not work, then the organ procurement agencies
would pretty much be out of business.

There is a constant need for public education. There is a need to make sure that organ and tissue procurement groups are held accountable to the public, which is represented by lawmakers who are elected to protect the rights of the citizens they serve. It would only be fair to say there is a need for organ and tissue donation in all of our communities. It is important that we are armed with the information to make an intelligent and timely decision. The public should feel comfortable in knowing that the donation process can proceed without causing premature deaths of innocent people. At the same time that we are approaching people to donate organs, the need to practice safe health guidelines, such as proper nutrition and regular exercise to take care of our bodies, should be discussed.

We should be teaching preventative measures to reduce the need for organ donations and transplantation at the same time that we talk about the need to donate. Let's talk about taking care of ourselves. I want to be sure that those individuals who have not had access to healthcare their entire lives are not going to be the ones first asked to donate organs and tissue. We have to ensure that the system is fair, that it treats people with equality and respect. Hopefully, one day these presumed consent laws will be abolished by the public. I hope we put education and more access to healthcare in their place.

Physicians and scientists are rushing into the laboratories at this point and time to experiment with cloning of individuals. Many are realizing that until we are able to clone tissue and organs, there will be a tremendous need for donated tissues and organs, which can help save lives. I know the need for donations is great. It is greater in the minority communities and in the areas where people do not have access to health care, or the best living conditions, and suffer more from early morbidity (illness) and mortality (death) from diseases. Until we balance our health care systems in this country, we are going to have to fight the notion that people continue to feel as though they are going to be denied healthcare on the basis of their socioeconomic level or the color of their skin.

What can be done? We can arm ourselves with information. We can practice better daily routines to prevent some of these avoidable diseases like high blood pressure and kidney failure. We can also ask our legislators to look out for our best interest. Even though presumed consent is the law, it is a painful thing when a family realizes that donation was out of their control all along. There is no reason to hesitate to donate when you have the facts.

Death With Dignity

There are many times when our senior citizens become ill and, having suffered a complication of a disease or serious injury, seem to become medical experiments. In every orifice you will find tubes, electrodes, and catheters. Sometimes these patients have agony on their faces. It is painful for me to watch. I interact with a lot of senior citizens and they are always quite concerned about their future and their quality of life as they age. Many times these individuals will ask me what will happen to them as they grow older and become sickly. Sometimes they will state, "I do not want to end up in your office." I reply to them very honestly, "If you do not want to end up in my office, then there are things that you must do, and do now."

If indeed someone has died a traumatic or unnatural death, then according to the law, an examination must be done in the medical examiner's office to determine the cause and manner of death. If the person has died and there is no evidence that foul play has occurred, and there is a strong documented history of chronic illness or disease, and if the proper paperwork has been completed, there will be no need to have that individual's body brought to the medical examiner's office. These issues are rarely attended to and many senior citizens, upon their deaths, end up at the medical examiner's office mainly because no one knew the person's medical history or no one knew how to get in touch with a family member or a physician. A great deal of the time, the reason that medical examiners investigate deaths of senior citizens is because they lived alone and, sadly, died alone. In this situation, I cannot help but think of my grandparents and be grateful that they did not die alone.

Many do not realize that anybody twenty-one or older can make out an advance directive. This document directs what the individual wants done in case he or she is no longer able to make decisions for themselves. This is an important document to have completed and have it either in your personal possessions or share it with your physician, minister, adult child, or caregiver. The document should be easily accessible in your home or hospital room, or you should have directions to locate it in your safety deposit box. Having a completed directive allows medical personnel to understand the patient's decision and wishes. Having an advance directive can ease prolonging treatment in some of the extreme cases where the patient has lost his ability to communicate with family or a caregiver.

I think that it is a good idea for senior citizens to have something on their person that allows others to find out information about them, whether it is an identification band like Medic Alert, or even a pendant with a contact information source on it. It is so sad that many times my office receives bodies because the person did not have a personal physician to relate his medical history to us. The advance directive, when properly filled out and witnessed, should be followed by health professionals. A form can be obtained from your personal attorney, hospitals, or even in an office supply store. You want to make sure to have the document notarized or give it to someone in a position of authority or a confidante so that it can be found when necessary. Death with dignity is important to most patients, especially if they do not want heroic measures used when they lose their ability to communicate, cannot control their bodily functions, or no longer have a meaningful quality of life. It can be destructive to ignore these written requests of patients.

There is another sad component to death with dignity. I have observed this reaction most frequently with senior citizens facing impending death. Their adult children will many times plead with them not to leave or not to let go. I have learned to advise these well-intended, grieving children that sometimes you have to let go. It is not in our power to stop the death process. Sometimes you have to look your loved one in the eye, let the person know that you love him, make sure that he is comfortable, ask if he is ready to go and, if the person can answer yes, tell him that you understand

and to go in peace. It can be the worst feeling in the world to a person who is ready, particularly a senior adult who has lived a long life, full of quality, to feel that he must hang on because his loved ones are not strong enough to let him go. I believe that some of the reasons that our senior citizens commit suicide so frequently is because they want to end their life quickly. When a grieving family member is strong enough to let go of a person on the verge of death, it is often more peaceful for all parties.

Death with dignity worked with my grandmother who lived well into her nineties. Mama Hart, as I fondly called her, was the oldest surviving member of our family and I had talked about her death with her often. My grandmother had been quite active and she would always say to me, "Whatever happens, I do not want to live in a nursing home, I do not want to be kept alive by machines, and I do not want to live with my children." She would always say that she wanted to live on her own for as long as she could. She would look me in the eye and say, "You make sure that if I cannot take care of myself that I am not put into a nursing home."

As Mama Hart began to become seriously ill with multiorgan system failure, as many of our seniors do, my mother relocated to my grandmother's hometown to take care of her. I often observed my own mother saying to Mama Hart, "Don't you leave me," and I would always say to her, "Mother, when the time comes, we have to let her go." My mother and I have never had the same feelings about death, with my accepting it and her fearing it. As time passed and Mama Hart became worse and needed to be hospitalized, she reminded me of the promise that I made to her. Just a few months before my grandmother passed away she called me to come visit her. We had a wonderful weekend together. We talked about her history, her childhood, her beliefs, her strengths, and it was a good visit. At the end of the weekend, I asked "Are you ready to go on?" She said, "Yes, I am ready to go on, so when the time comes I am ready to go to meet the angels." Hearing her say that made me sad, but I realized that she had lived a wonderful life, she had spent most of it without pain, she had raised children, and she was now bearing witness to great-great-grandchildren, and I knew that when the time came I would find the strength to celebrate her home going. A few months went by and my mother was becoming very upset because Mama Hart was visibly failing. There was a time when my grandmother was in and out of consciousness during her last days and I would observe my own mother crying and pleading with my grandmother again, "Please don't leave us, we are not ready for you go to." One day my mother called me and she said, "I was in your grandmother's room saying my sad woes and begging her not to go, and a nurse walked by and she came in and said, 'No, let me tell you what to say.' The nurse, a perfect stranger, said to my mother, take your mother's hand and tell her, 'It is okay, you have raised me well, I can carry on and I love you.' I told my mother, "That is right, let her go. You are a grown woman, and she did raise you well; she raised you to be strong. Let her go in peace. She is ready to go, in fact, she has been ready to go, just let her go." Shortly after, Mama Hart died peacefully and it was much easier for the family to deal with, knowing that it was her desire to go on quietly in this way.

Do not let your elderly loved one die with a sense of guilt! Look at death as transformation, particularly when the person has lived long enough to become an angel on earth. That is what I call senior citizens, angels on earth, because they have lived enough to benefit from all the wisdom of their collective years. There is a sense of calmness and serenity in their expressions. There has been an acceptance of their end of life that is to be envied. This attitude is death with dignity. Grieving survivors feel alone when we have lost a loved one, particularly when they have held the family together, because we are left behind. We do not know where they have gone. We only know that we can no longer see them or touch them. We must trust that they have gone to a better place. There will be a vacancy for the rest of our lives but we will know they have passed into another realm in a peaceful manner.

While performing my internship in New York City, I encountered a woman who asked me to help her find death with dignity. At that time, in the early 1980s, there were a lot of laws concerning terminal healthcare and they were quite strict in the State of New York. Doctors could not lawfully participate in ending a patient's life, something with which I continue to morally agree. However, there still existed the possibility of respecting the Hippocratic oath of doing no harm and respecting the patient's wishes. This particular woman was a middle-aged white female with a grown daughter in her late twenties.

The older female was my patient and she was suffering from metastatic breast cancer. She admitted to me that she had felt a lump in her breast about three years prior to being diagnosed with the disease. She had done nothing about it. She said that she had wished it away and the lump only got bigger and the problem grew worse. By the time she went to the doctor to have the diagnosis confirmed, it was too late. The cancerous growth had begun to erode through the skin of her right breast and had spread to the left one. Her only choice of treatment at that time was to undergo a radical mastectomy, chemotherapy, and radiation therapy. This woman was in the peak of her life, and she had undergone such extensive therapy that she had lost her strength. The tumor was unable to be controlled and had continued to spread. By the time I became her physician she presented to the hospital with metastases to her skeletal bone and to her brain. She had been admitted to my medical service for palliative chemotherapy. She was a sweet, good-natured woman and I often sat and talked with her, holding her hand. Some days all she wanted to do was just talk. She had a poignant story to tell and she asked me to help her tell it. I am.

One day this brave lady turned to me and asked what I could do for her when her time came. She asked me if I would speak with her and her daughter in confidence and, of course, I agreed. The session was quite tearful and emotional. Her daughter expressed the same request, that if something happened and her mother took a turn for the worse, that her mother be allowed to die in peace with dignity. I promised that I would do all that I could do to assure that this would happen while upholding the laws of the State of New York. I had given my word and I meant to keep it. A few days later, my patient coughed up some material and called for me. I knew that the time of her death was very close. I reminded her that she could depend on me, day or night. I urged her that if anything happened and I was not in the hospital to please have someone page me, and I would be right there. Luckily I lived close to the hospital and I could get there within two to three minutes.

Sure enough, just thirty-six hours later, I was on call at the hospital and my patient began to take a turn for the worse and I was paged to her room. She was still alert and her daughter was at her side. Both of these women were crying. The patient was short of breath and she asked me to help her, and her daughter to accept her death. I replied to her that the only thing that we could do was pray. I then shut the door to the room and the three of us held hands and we began to pray. We prayed for thankfulness. We thanked God for this lady giving birth to her daughter and raising her. We prayed for her daughter's strength. We prayed for all of the other women who may suffer from this type of cancer and lack of knowledge. Together we all prayed for the strength to allow this lady to be able to pass on to another world with dignity. About twenty minutes went by and we continued to pray and to hug one another. We all cried and kept holding hands, then the patient died. But she died understanding that she was not going to be tortured anymore from medical treatment.

She died with her child next to her, and she died knowing that I had kept my promise. It was painful but there was some relief in knowing that we had carried out her wishes. It was a matter of listening to a patient and allowing what was possible to happen without complications. Many may argue that this was not medically ethical but I believe that I carried out the Hippocratic oath, to do no harm. I believe that death with dignity is possible but it requires two things: communication and respect for life.

No Deposit, No Return

As an examiner of the dead, I study all kinds of injuries, diseases, and accidents that claim the lives of young people and healthy adults. Many of the deaths I investigate are due to the abuse of one's own precious gift. That gift is our body, which includes our health. Too many people die prematurely as a result of obesity and poor nutrition. Illnesses such as heart diseases, kidney failure, liver failure, diabetes mellitus (sugar), hypertension (high blood pressure), and infections are rooted in poor nutrition and poor eating habits.

Many of us have lost the ability to recognize that water is not only our most precious resource but absolutely essential to living well. Too many children are started off drinking juice and other sweet things and are not given enough water. These children do not develop a taste for water as youngsters and, therefore, resist water consumption when they are adults. Our body weight is approximately sixty percent water. We need to drink water every day. People shudder when they think about needing to drink eight glasses of water a day. In reality, if you monitor what most people drink per day, they are consuming more than eight glasses of soda, tea, juice or coffee. We must be trained to put back into our body what we take out. Not only do we lose water through urination but also through our tears and sweat; just keeping our body functioning uses up water. If everybody learned as a child to drink a cup of water for every waking hour, we would be a much more hydrated, healthy population.

I am convinced that the basis of high blood pressure in our society is our lack of water intake combined with too much salt in our diets. Most people do not realize that the normal blood pressure is not 120/80 millimeters of mercury (mmHg). The blood pressure could be much lower. The blood pressure of a newborn infant is approximately 90/60. The 120/80 blood pressure is an average figure that is listed as normal. It becomes normal because we have allowed the inclusion of salt in our diet. Salt was a natural additive several decades ago as a way to get iodine into our diets. It certainly has value but we have learned to live on a diet with too much of it. Look at all of the canned and dried food as well as cured meat, and examine the salt content. Many people are so used to having excessive salt in their diet that they do not recognize the natural flavor of food without salt. I observe people when they are out dining. There are people who will begin to sprinkle large amounts of salt or pepper before they even smell or taste the dish. Some of us do not recognize the true flavor of vegetables or bread because we immediately apply additives such as butter or salt. Human beings are brought into this world with enough salt in our bodies to last us. All we have to do is maintain some balance.

When you think about preparation you must question what is being added to our food. Currently, with the leaning toward cloning and other scientific ways to improve upon our population, it is slowly coming to light that we have long been the subjects of an undisclosed study of chemical additives to our food supply. It is my belief that in the long run, the health of our population will reveal the direct effect of food additives on the morbidity and mortality of our society. Most of us do not even know what we are eating. Gone are the days when the cow and pig were butchered on the family farm and processed then and there. Currently, our government allows so many chemicals and antibiotics to be added to our chicken and meat-producing animals we do not realize what a normal chicken looks like anymore. If you are fortunate to go to the country and see free range animals you will notice how much smaller and leaner they are. When you go to the supermarket and look at the meat being sold, you have to wonder what kind of colossal chicken produced those gigantic legs and wings. There have been questions raised about why our children are larger and maturing physically and sexually at younger ages. Could it be the hormones that have been added to our food? After all, the food chain filters down at some point. There should be more education about healthy diets and awareness of what additives are allowed to be put into our food.

Milk and dairy products are foods that I, personally, do not consume much. I happen to be one of those African-Americans who do not digest milk products well. I am not against dairy farmers, however, I always wondered what nature really intended. As I analyze my own lactase insufficiency, I wonder if, perhaps, I have been fighting Mother Nature. I, too, was raised to drink milk. I just never liked the look and taste of whole milk. I remember questioning why we humans drank milk. Every other milk-producing animal uses its milk for the nourishment and protection of the newborn. I believe that children should be breast-fed for at least the first several months of life. Breast milk confers immunity from the mother to the child until the child's system kicks in for protection against infection. I can think of no other animal that naturally has a lifelong dependency on milk.

To take it a step farther, it has always seemed unnatural to be drinking another animal's milk. I wonder that if we were to replace milk with life-giving water, if it would be less detrimental to our systems. I realize that we have a need for calcium and that a lot of tasty things can be made with dairy products. Is our need to drink milk natural or is it because there is an industry that depends upon selling milk?

Another issue that comes to mind as far as our nutritional habits are concerned is vitamin and food supplements. The basic food groups, which consist of fruit and vegetables, meats and fish, dairy and grains, are enough, if eaten properly. Then again, we have the other two groups, sugar and fats, that are so commonly used to tease us.

We have become a society engrossed with fat and greasy fast food. We are a people who are on the move with no time for breakfast or dinner. I see people who have abused their bodies for years begin to swallow handfuls of supplemental drugs, not fully understanding the effect that these chemicals could have on their body. The word *vitamin* itself means little bits. We would receive an adequate amount of vitamins if we ate the proper foods regularly.

Since most people do not have good nutritional habits, the industry of supplements is going strong. Rarely, do you see an ad that shows fresh natural vegetables that are not smothered with fattening salad dressing or gooey butter. I am so tired of hearing commercials where church choirs sing about chicken and artificial biscuits, I could scream! It is as if we should not take the time to eat properly. We cannot make up the twenty to thirty years of abuse with a handful of pills and capsules. Some of the bodies that I examine look as if the person has lived twice as long because of the dietary abuse. We do not teach people to take care of their bodies.

There is definitely a nutritional basis to many of our diseases, and our unhealthy eating habits add up to early mortality. People who drink alcohol and overindulge in fatty foods starve themselves of proper nutrition. Many of those who drink alcohol and fail to eat end up with nutritional diseases such as cirrhosis of the liver, gastrointestinal bleeding, premature heart disease, central nervous system dysfunction, and skin problems. There are empty calories in alcohol. Alcohol has no nutritional value other than to make us feel good or lose our inhibitions for a short while. The exception is the consideration of red wine and women's health, but my focus here is on excessive consumption of alcoholic beverages.

Too much of a good thing becomes a vicious cycle. Not only do we have an industry that sells products to people who can least afford the side effects, but we do the same thing with our food. Poor people are under attack in this country! Look at where the highest concentration of fast-food restaurants and liquor stores are and the least amount of green space and fresh food items are. The same people have little or limited access to medical treatment and prevention. There is no wonder why they also have little faith in the medical community. From my viewpoint this is no less planned than sequential traffic lights on the streets. We must stop the personal violence!

Education may be the only way to change these habits. But, of course, we have allowed the education in the public realm to falter, particularly in the inner city. We have weakened the public education system in inner-city neighborhoods in order to promote diversity in the suburban schools. These same students from the inner city and poor neighborhoods or rural areas start out with poor nutrition, then they fall into another cycle. For instance, some poor students have no breakfast, which makes it difficult to concentrate in school. In some places students are then diagnosed with attention deficit disorder or put in special education classes. In short, they are branded and do not receive the necessary benefits of public education.

Too much of a good thing becomes a vicious cycle. Not only do we have an industry that sells products to people who can least afford the side effects, we do the same thing with our food. Poor people are under attack in this country! Look at where the highest concentration of fast-food restaurants and liquor stores are and the least amount of green space and fresh food items are. These same people have little or limited access to medical treatment and prevention. There is no wonder why they also have little faith in the medical community. From my viewpoint this is no less planned than sequential traffic lights on the streets. We must stop the personal violence!

Our forefathers ate heavy and fat-laden diets but they also worked more physically challenging jobs. Our society has changed and so must our eating habits. We must find a way to get back to eating more balanced diets with lower caloric intake. It makes no sense to have the added pressure of ads that draw our population out to consume more heavy, high caloric, unhealthy food.

There is another dangerous factor to consider. Instant weight loss is upon us. This has become the new multi-billion dollar industry. Instant weight loss runs the gamut from early-morning fake infomercials selling gimmicky exercise machines to starvation liquid meals. If it took months and years to gain the weight, why would anyone believe a slim model/actress who claims to have lost fifty pounds in one month? People believe it because they need to. These ads, gimmicks, pills, powders, and potions are playing upon a person's desire to change his body image in order to fit into our weight-conscious society. These products that are being sold over and under the counter and through the airwaves are producing huge profits that are going into someone's pocket.

I have received so many ads telling me that I can wake up ten pounds lighter. I suppose I could if I kept opening my wallet! The best exercise is still walking or swimming and ultimately pushing back from the table. Treat your body like the temple it was meant to be. We could all benefit from returning to some of our basics. The key to good health is like the old glass soda bottles; no deposit, no return.

It is Not A Question Of What If

I highly recommend that individuals set aside a time to discuss the issue of *what if* with their family members. This is particularly important for individuals who have immediate family such as spouses or children, or single, separated, or divorced people who may have elderly parents or dependents. It is important that we take the time to think about the consequences of somebody dying without having the proper paperwork completed. We do not like to think of a person whom we love dying but if one should die without having a will, an insurance policy, or even bank accounts identified, the surviving family members will be in a quandary. So many families have to search for these personal papers while planning for a funeral that I feel compelled to emphasize this topic.

Because death is seldom of our choosing, many people die without having made out a will or the will cannot be located. There is no way for the family to tell what their loved one would have wanted to be done with their body or how they would want their savings or worldly possessions dispersed. It may not be possible to even close certain accounts or to get bank accounts in order. It must be considered part of the responsibility of having a family or a business to seek guidance from an attorney, accountant, or an insurance agent. You may even seek guidance from your religious leader, but the planning needs to be done. Some single people do not make out wills or designate someone to close their business affairs. These same suggestions are relevant to the single person, even for the care of their pets. We all have individuals to whom we are attached, whether they are blood family or friends.

It is equally important that paperwork lend itself toward the division of property, assets, and advance directives about medical care be discussed with those you consider important. So many times families will come to me after death has occurred bewildered and indecisive about what to do, even for the funeral and burial. The most common thing that I hear is, "I do not know what he would have wanted. We had never talked about it."

As a single person, I have made sure to write a will and to outline the items that I have accrued during my lifetime involving my work and writing, as well as personal possessions I would like to be distributed to those who can best use them. For example, I have made arrangements to have my pathology material sent to Howard University where I received my education, and for which I retain much fondness. I know this material will be taken care of and it will be used. My pathology photo collection is useless to my family who would not only *not* understand its use, but would not really want these pictures around the house. It just makes sense. Even though it was not a popular topic, I have discussed with my mother what I would like to have done should I pass away before her. It is something that had to be talked about. Although unpleasant to deal with, once you have the discussion and you know what the other individual would want, you will have more peace of mind, because those desires will be met in the future. I know how my family and friends would react in the event of my death, so I have taken the responsible position of addressing some of these questionable issues beforehand.

There are other individuals who have taken the time to write a Last Will and Testament or advance directives for terminal medical care, but they have not shared the location of those documents. There may be a hunt for the location of said items, if they are looked for at all, when death occurs. Not only do you have to write the documents, you have to tell somebody where they are or how to locate them in the event of your untimely death. You have to make sure that the proper person will have access to the documents and that the documents will be held in a secure place.

It is important that families communicate in this realistic way because, in this day, there are only rare occasions when our entire family gathers. Most of the time we come together for celebrations, weddings, childbirth, or graduation. However, there are other occasions when the families only gather when tragedy has occurred. Unfortunately, sadness, illness, and death have a way of bringing more people together than perhaps it should.

We all know the reality of death exists. If we would all just learn to slow down and take life a little easier, perhaps we would be able to deal with death when it occurs. We should just take the opportunity to live life and enjoy it; to call people because we want to hear from them, not because we have to; to visit people because we miss them; not when it is too late. Death is not a question of *what if*, it is a question of when, and will we be prepared to deal with the situation?

When The Call Comes

On the morning that I was preparing to give what I considered the greatest antismoking talk of my young career, I was disturbed, uneasily, from sleep. It was about five o'clock on April 6, 1981. I reached over, fumbled, and grabbed the phone in the dark. "Is this Joye Carter?" the voice on the telephone asked. I replied, "Yes." The next sentence changed my outlook on death notification forever. The nameless voice on the other end of the telephone did not identify himself but simply continued on in a rapid monotone and said, "Your father is dead and we would like to do an autopsy." I did not know what was worse, the news that my father was dead and that I was not at his side when he passed or the way the notification had been made about his death. I did not receive an, "I am sorry," or "This is Dr. so and so, and I have some bad news to tell you." Just those cold words, "Your father is dead and we would like to do an autopsy." I immediately replied "No, I do not want an autopsy performed on my father's body. We know what he died of and it was his wish not to have an autopsy and I must honor his wishes."

I hung up the phone, and my first thought was, *my goodness, that is a terrible way to inform a person that a loved one has died.* I asked myself, *who was that person? Why would you call a patient's family first thing in the morning and deliver such horrible news without even finding out the condition of the person that you were speaking with?* As I replayed that conversation in my mind, I began to realize that the person who called me was probably more afraid of notifying me of the death than I was to hear it. After all, I realized that my father was gravely ill. I knew that his condition was very serious. But when it is someone you love, someone you have called upon over the years who has always been a strong and leading force in your life, it is difficult to believe you will never see that person or feel his touch again. As I got out of bed, I kept thinking about that scared voice on the phone and the crude method used to inform me. I then wondered if that was what I was going to be doing as a physician. *Was I going to have that kind of coarse interaction with families? Did the person who called me care about my feelings?* I made up my mind that I would never give the news about death to a family member in that way.

When I got up from my bed and went into the bathroom and reality hit me, I was unable to cry. My father was gone and I had not been able to hold his hand and tell him that I loved him one more time. It was then that I looked into the mirror and noticed the first streak of gray hair extending from the left side of my forehead all the way back. It had happened in an instant. I felt then that part of my father's soul had passed through me and changed my life forever. I also felt numb, as if someone had poured ice water all over me. I was slightly dazed and not fully in control of my emotions. I knew that I had to keep on moving.

I went ahead and prepared to go to school that day because I had to. I could not just stay home and cry. I had to complete my school assignment. Since I was awakened so early I was able to arrive for medical school early. I located one of my professors, Calvin Sampson, M.D., and told him my father had died that morning but I felt even more compelled to give this talk about emphysema, because it was smoking that had killed my father. I told him if he did not mind I would like to give the presentation and then go home. Dr.

Sampson said that he understood. Then I asked him

not to tell my classmates until I had given my

presentation because I needed to get through my

talk. Dr. Sampson promised me that he would not

betray my confidence and I felt calmer knowing I

would be able to speak my peace without the

emotional impact interfering with my words.

I passed through the first part of the morning

in a daze. I did not want anyone to know about my

father's death and I did not want anyone to feel

sorry for me. I just knew I had to get through

pathology class. Finally, the time came for the

discussion. Our group showed a pair of lungs that

were healthy and pink to the rest of the class. We

showed a pair of lungs that were black and

shriveled from chronic infectious disease. Then we

showed a pair of lungs that were distorted due to

emphysema with lots of scar tissue and dilated air chambers. Our group discussed diseases caused by cigarette smoking and the mechanisms that are interfered with when you have destruction of lung tissue. Then it was my turn to discuss the pathology. I discussed and showed slides about the effects of smoking and related diseases on the lungs. I demonstrated how carbon pigment became embedded in the lung tissue and never fully cleared out. I described how the air spaces became dilated and distorted. I remember showing lots of pictures about smoking. After I finished my show-and-tell, I told my classmates that my father was a typical example of a person addicted to tobacco. I closed my discussion by saying, "And he died this morning. No one knows better than me at this time how devastating cigarettes are."

After hearing those solemn words my classmates were in shock themselves and did not know how to respond. Finally one of my female classmates came up to me and put her arms around me and gave me a big hug. She told me her daddy died because he was addicted to alcohol and she knew what I was going through. At that point, I began to cry. I had gotten through my speech and I had been stoic for as long as I could. I had given my message with an impact and then I had to let go. As I cried, I thought maybe it would be best if I left medical school. Maybe I knew too much, that's why it hurt so much. Then I thought about my father and how proud he was of me getting into medical school and I knew that he would not have wanted me to quit. He would want me to finish and do what I needed to do. He would want me to keep spreading the word about diseases and how we could live healthier lives. And so, I have devoted my personal and professional time to educating the community about the effects of tobacco and alcohol.

I admonish my staff to be courteous and helpful when they have to notify a family that one of their relatives has died. Whenever possible, we try to make that notice in person and not over the telephone.

Even if your loved one is known to have a non-survivable injury or disease, the finality of the death pronouncement is monumental. Because of my own experiences I can understand what families and friends go through when abrupt death announcements have been made. The emotional suffering and sense of loss is even greater when the death is sudden or violent.

The cruel fact is that we never know when the call will come. I can only hope that we as physicians and health-care providers can do our part to make that call less painful.

What's Love Got To Do With It?

It is a sad thing to realize that sometimes the words to a popular song have a deeper meaning than anybody first realized. When I use the phrase or question, "What's love got to do with it?" I am referring to a category of death that may develop in domestic living situations. There may not necessarily be a criminal history of domestic violence in the perpetrator's background. These types of deaths may occur in relationships as formal as thirty years of marriage or as little as two to three weeks of going together. Sometimes one of the individuals is not able to cope with or accept the breakup of the relationship and the other person moving on. The "Till death do us part" becomes literal. One of the people in the relationship cannot go on and refuses to allow a former lover, the object of his affection, to go on as well. On most of these occasions there is at least one homicide and one suicide of a paired death that must be investigated.

In many of these domestic cases the person who cannot move on decides to take the life of the person for whom he continues to have strong feelings, as well as, anybody else in that person's life, whether it be the person's children, a new love, or even another family member such as a mother, father, brother, or sister-in-law. I have investigated cases where one spouse killed another in front of the children and cases where everyone was killed. In many of these situations, these murders were unpredictable. There are also a great number of cases where the fatal outcome was predicted. Many of the latter cases have histories of police reports and previous law enforcement calls to the home prior to the homicide.

You may not know at which point the person you said "I do" to and exchanged rings with will be unable to cope with changes in the relationship. Unfortunately, many marriages and relationships do not last. Even though the couples have gone through a legal separation or divorce and time has passed, one person may still show signs of being unable to move on. Sometimes it is the result of seeing a former lover with a new person or a wedding that sets off something in the perpetrator's psyche that was unpredicted.

Domestic violence homicides are often some of the most unsettling death cases to investigate. There is no logic in the killing; it is all emotional.

In some parts of the country, many medical examiners refer to these types of deaths as 'divorces'. I have heard terms such as Mexican divorce, Cuban divorce, or black divorce, and I find none of these terms funny. Oftentimes the comments become stereotypical remarks that are made when one gets too comfortable and lacks sensitivity for the community being served. I have found these types of fatal domestic violence cases to occur in all ethnic groups. It does not matter about the color of the victim's skin. What matters is that there is some emotional imbalance or dependency that has developed in one person involved in the relationship. That person feels that he or she cannot live without their former mate or cannot accept that the other partner has moved on and is now happy with somebody else.

It is not always that the perpetrator was jealous when he killed another person. He does not always show signs or tendencies toward jealousy. The violence can be sudden and it can be terrorizing. Sometimes these homicides represent the phrase that you can never know another person one hundred percent. What concerns me, as a medical examiner, is that these types of homicide cases appear to be on the rise, while drive-by, acquaintance shootings are on the decline. Currently, in Texas, and many other states, there appears to be more homicide/suicide deaths arising out of domestic situations than in previous years.

What is unexplained and discomforting to the general public is how these types of murders can occur when a couple who has been married for thirty years suddenly has a fight, but no one predicted a fatal outcome. I have no magic glasses. I can only try to educate. Sometimes, unfortunately, there are records of prior reports to law enforcement that were not taken seriously. There is no way to predict if somebody will make good on a threat.

All anyone can do for those who are left behind is sympathize with them and take comfort in the fact that the mourned loved one can no longer be hurt. As some people have told me, when I was in the middle of investigating a homicide/suicide case, they knew who did it. Occasionally, the scene is questionable as to who killed whom. The homicide/suicide scenario is the general outcome when the person who feels incapable of moving on killed the person who was the object of his affection and then killed himself. Oftentimes, the surviving family members will tell me that at least the murderer took his or her own life, which saved the emotional toll of going through a drawn-out court proceeding. To those who have suffered from this type of violence, there are no words that will make the hurt go away. It may be good for you to know that there are others out there who have experienced what you are going through. Perhaps you may take comfort in knowing that other people are dealing with the same type of grief.

There is something about our current younger generation that underscores the notion that no matter how fast-paced our society is or how widely we travel, there will be some people who just cannot make it on their own. It is a pity when a younger couple breaks up and no longer is a pair, that both people cannot go on leading their individual lives. There is no way to decide which situation is sadder: a couple who has been together many years or a couple who could have grown old together had they been suited to each other. How do you make a choice between a person who kills his mate in a burst of anger or two young people who have not experienced all that life has to offer who end up with the same tragic result? For either couple it is a terrible outcome.

It is particularly sad when young people feel they can no longer carry on because the "love" of their life has spurned them. This type of fatality is another opportunity where I think a strong role-model adult figure could have let them know that we all go through ups and downs in relationships and somehow we survive. In other words, the ones we chose to love do not always love us back. Many of these young people who have ended relationships through homicide/suicide did not believe they had the strength to survive on their own. It is not for me to say why these deaths occur. I do not have that much wisdom but, unfortunately, I have too much experience. It seems to be that in our fast-paced world we are all trying to hang on to just a little bit of love and a little bit of humanity. When that emotional support is taken away, some of us find that we cannot stand on our own. Perhaps, this type of domestic violence is a call for more life-skills training in our schools, more premarital relationship counseling and, maybe, just more time out! It is sad to say that domestic violence is now occurring with increasing frequency. Violence is violence! To answer the question posed in the title of this chapter, love has nothing to do with it. Maybe more self-love would prevent this type of self-destruction.

Facts of Life

As a physician and medical examiner I am obligated to uphold the law. Many times the law, my upbringing, and my beliefs clash. One of the more frequent occurrences is the topic of abortion. As a Christian, it is my belief that life begins when the sperm and egg unite. When those organisms merge, that is a creation of life I feel only God can cause to happen. However, under the guidelines of which I work, I must uphold the legal aspect of death investigation and put my personal feelings aside.

The current law, which is based upon federal regulations, states in general terms that a fetus (while in the mother's womb) does not exist until one breath is taken independent of his mother. This is actually the basis for determining whether or not there has been a live birth or a stillbirth. If just one breath is taken, then a fetus is called an infant and the delivery is termed a live birth. If no breath is taken and the fetus is delivered with no movement, then it is a stillbirth. It stands to reason that if you have not been born, you cannot die. These are the laws, and currently they appear quite antiquated compared to today's technology and medical procedures. For example, the medical examiner will be asked to evaluate a pregnant woman's death or the death of a fetus after a pregnant woman has been injured. This becomes a problematic case for a person such as myself. The woman, upon examination, looks very pregnant but has died from trauma or disease. In these types of investigations and postmortem examinations pathologists not only examine the female body but must also examine the fully formed identifiable fetus, complete with every tissue and body part recognizable as that of a newborn infant. Under the current law, because that fetus remained inside of the woman's body and did not take a breath, it is not considered a human being. Even when the pregnant woman has been assaulted or is in a traffic accident, only one person has died. Only one human life will be documented as far as the manner of death of a pregnant woman in situations like these. The legal question has been answered but not the moral question.

Another situation occurs if there has been injury to the mother and the fetus is delivered prematurely. Several years ago a premature fetus under the gestational age of twenty-six weeks would probably not have survived. Due to the advances in science and technology, this is no longer the common outcome. Healthcare providers have come such a long way in our neonatology and intensive care abilities that many of these fetuses are taken right from the womb, by cesarean section or natural birth, and are placed immediately on a ventilator where the machine breathes for them. Thanks to technology and wonderful medical care, many of these premature infants survive. For those infants who do not survive, the medical examiner will become involved in the investigation if trauma caused the injury to the mother. These types of cases leave forensic pathologists in a legal quandary. Legally, a fetus that is removed from the mother and immediately put on life support has not officially taken an independent breath. Under the current federal law the fetus should not exist as a human being. Medically, when these infants have survived for minutes, hours, or days, they must be given a death certificate. You can see where the problem lies. It is time once again for lawmakers and physicians to come together and review how technology has changed the way we examine life, as well as death.

Another area where I must balance my response, as a physician and as a woman, concerns the aborted fetus. I recall looking at these perfectly formed tiny human bodies presented to me in containers during my residency in surgical pathology at Howard University Hospital. The medical term is called abortion when the fetal remains are removed from the woman's womb as a medical procedure. I often look at these miniature human forms in amazement. How tiny we all began! Sometimes I would feel a pang of emotional pain to realize that this being, for some reason or another, would not have an opportunity at life. This is always a problematic situation when you believe life begins at the union of sperm and egg. This feeling, however, is juxtaposed to the one that I suffer when I see newborn babies and older infants who have been thrown away after birth with no more consideration than garbage. Imagine being carried in the mother's uterus for nine months, where it was safe and secure and then being discarded in nothing more than a used grocery bag. I often ask myself what I would rather investigate, an unwanted child whose life ended before it began or an unwanted child whose life began and then ended abruptly? Both of these human beings are innocent. It is always more difficult to examine the body of a full-term infant who has taken a breath and perhaps looked around at the world through its small eyes. This is when you have to put your personal feelings aside and carry out your medical and legal responsibilities.

Many pregnancies are hidden and emotionally painful. As adults, we realize that we can not go back to undo what has been done, but the investigation of child death begs the question; when you find the body of an infant perhaps one, two, or three months old who survived the birth process, who was born into this world to a woman, who was cared for, and then all of a sudden thrown away, the death investigator wonders why somebody stopped caring. Somebody threw the child out, or harmed him like it did not matter anymore. The child was killed and discarded. When a person purposely harms a child, I feel strongly. If you do not want your baby, please hand him over to someone or take him to a place where he will be found by people and loved. Do not throw your child out in the trash! Do not leave your child out in the cold! Somebody could find that infant and love him and raise him. If you are going to carry a child for nine months, then do the right thing. I am glad to say now that there are laws that will allow a mother, who feels she cannot take care of her child, to leave him in a public place where he can be found without being exposed to the elements.

Sometimes I know that young women cannot help their circumstances. Whether it is a matter of ignorance or the outcome of unprotected sexual intercourse, the fear of parental influence, or realizing that once the birth of a child has occurred you are not emotionally or financially equipped to manage the situation, the unwanted child deserves to live. Please, I beg of you, on behalf of that infant to call someone in confidence, take that child to a hospital, police station, or another public place. Have someone come and care for the child. Please do not discard our children. Think of the child. He did not ask to be born.

I believe that it is the right of a woman to choose. I also feel strongly that a woman must realize she is choosing for two. It is important that we, as physicians, take a greater role in educating the community, especially young people, about life and when it begins.

We may think that sex education is wrong but if more adults acted as role models and started talking to teenagers as if they were young adults we might have fewer infants who end up in the medical examiner's office needing postmortem evaluation. Hopefully, there will be fewer children and infants who end up discarded like old vegetables. I believe that we must teach young people to abstain. If they are not going to abstain then we must arm them with the facts of life. Not only about how life begins and the result of sexual intercourse but also the fact that there are health problems associated with unprotected sex, as well as the increased risk

of certain types of cancer.

We know that premature sexual activity can

affect a young person's emotional development. As

a physician, I do not believe a child is too young to

understand about the birds and the bees. Of course

there is a different format that you would use for an

elementary school pupil than you would for a junior

high student. If you think children today do not

know what is going on, take a walk in their little

gym shoes for a while. There are so many sexual

innuendoes in our cartoons, comic books, PG-rated

movies and television shows, that adults would

learn something new if they paid attention. If we as

parents and role models laugh, snicker and act

embarrassed when providing sexual education and

information, then we are not offering a solid base

for our young people to make good decisions. We

must help young people make informed decisions they can feel good about.

It is sad to hear parents say that they do not want their child to learn about sex. I dare these same parents to go into the schoolyard to hear what is being said. I would rather young people be armed with correct information than misinformed. It is difficult to keep your child inside a vacuum these days and it is difficult to keep a child innocent for long in today's world. Our society moves a whole lot faster than it did when I was a girl. We have to be aware as parents and teachers that the world has changed from the time when we were all children. The parents I know who speak openly with their children have better lines of communication, and their children have healthier outlooks about their own bodies and sexuality than those who have not taken the time to have those parent/child conversations.

One of my great fears is that those individuals who annually and consistently protest the Rowe vs. Wade decision would one day get their way and overturn abortion. I fear that we will be right back where we started in the 1960s with those deadly back-alley abortions. I remember them and I have witnessed the fatal outcomes more than a few times during the span of my forensic pathology career. I fear this happening again, when women feel they no longer have the choice over the function of their bodies. While it is not my call to decide if a person should have the ability to end the life of another begun through carnal knowledge, it would be a travesty to return to the era when women had no choices. To have women and their unborn fetuses dying of toxic poisonings, infections, and massive blood loss from the use of hangers and other gross implements is a frightening thought. It is my desire that we as a society should move forward in a spirit of more open communication about choices.

It is a bit perplexing when I learn that a few people who protest abortion rights have no problem blowing up abortion clinics and killing people. To me, two wrongs do not make a right. Many of the same individuals who protest abortion rights of women are not willing to fund orphanages, nor are they willing to give to charities to take care of these unfortunate, unwanted children. Moreover, in the name of pro-life, some will kill over what they believe. This is just as wrong. It does not serve a purpose. I do not understand this logic. Perhaps it should be a choice between the mother, the father, and the physician. Perhaps the world should just stay out of it. These issues are political and social questions and not for me to answer in this book or at any conceivable time in the future. The investigation of deaths due to abortion or abandonment in infants causes me, as a physician, to question my legal responsibilities over my moral objections as a spiritual person. These are provocative issues that I have continued to think and pray about. These are, after all, the facts of life. The mysteries of life have yet to be completely understood by man.

When A Child Dies

It is impossible to place a degree of importance on an individual's death because it all depends on who is being affected. No one should feel that his loved one's death is of any less importance than anybody else's. There are, however, certain cases that are more disturbing to professional death investigators. Most investigators and physicians will admit that there is nothing more difficult to investigate than the death of a child.

Out of all the cases that I have been privileged to work with, and the hundreds of death investigators with whom I have come into contact, no matter how seasoned the person, the violent death of an innocent child always has an impact. Some of these cases can make a grown man cry. When you witness so much death, destruction, and hatred repeatedly, you tend to expect certain occurrences. I have come to expect numerous media inquiries, repetitive questions, and increased advocate activities when a child has died. Unfortunately, after the first few weeks, the interest usually decreases. With some cases, there is no interest at all. I have been part of investigative teams where the family does not even show an interest. There are many times when the only thing the country reacts to in unison is the death of an innocent child. Usually, it is the violent death that provokes a community reaction, as is the case with child abduction-homicides.

It is a horrible thing for a parent to lose a child. It is no less difficult if the child that you brought in the world died of disease or succumbed to injury from an unexpected accident. The pain that all of these families feel is immeasurable.

I have dealt with many parents over the years who have lost a child to an act of violence and there is something brutally different about these situations. First of all, it must be acknowledged that for a parent to lose a child is not the natural order of life. We all expect children to outlive parents. When a violent death occurs it leaves the family grappling with the question, what happened? It sends a chill through the community who then asks, "Could this same thing happen to my child?" Some adults ask, "Could that have happened to me?" The outcry becomes, "How did this happen?" "Why did it happen?" The unanswerable question becomes, "Is it going to happen again?" Particularly when there is no one to blame or to be held accountable in the unwitnessed murder of a child.

In today's society a child's death through abduction or sexual assault is a real fear. We appear to have more predators of children among us than ever before. Is it because of our computers? Is it our fast-paced society? Is it because of the media portraying more sexual assaults and childhood abductions on TV and on the big screen? I do not know. Just like the investigator who works on these types of homicide cases, you want to rush home and gaze upon your own loved ones and maybe hug them a little tighter.

When I investigate the death of a child I can predict that one or both of the parents will ask, at some point in the investigation, "Did my child suffer?" Many times that is an unanswerable question. I want to always be honest, tactful, and comforting. I will reply yes on occasion, if there is physical evidence of torture. Sometimes there is evidence of a struggle. But, I must also add a caveat with that explanation saying that I cannot tell for how long the child struggled or suffered but I hope in my heart that it was short and that upon the death of the child all of that pain was eased.

I personally feel that when an innocent person is killed, particularly a child who had not had the opportunity to live long enough to even make enemies, to learn right from wrong, or even develop conscience thought, that these young victims immediately go to a special place in heaven. When death occurs at the hands of an unloving person, that pain and suffering immediately dissipates and their spirit is in a better place. There is no doubt the parents will ask, "Why me?" "Why my child?" "Why did God do this to me?" Many parents will ask, "Why is God angry with me? They will say that they are angry at themselves or with God. At this point of acceptance there is nothing anyone can say to really soothe them. We must give parents their space to begin to deal with the sad situation. We must understand that they have suffered a tremendous loss. There is nothing more disturbing to the investigator than to not be able to answer a parent's questions when a culprit is at large.

As a death investigator I do not always have answers because I accept death as something that cannot always be predict. We cannot always protect our children, as much as we love them, from becoming victims. I have thought many times that when a tragedy like a child's death occurs and it galvanizes a community, perhaps it is a reminder that a child's birth is a precious thing and we all need to be kinder to one another. We all need to appreciate one another while we can. My spirituality is what I use to deal with these difficult situations.

I have witnessed the biggest, strongest, most seasoned investigators crumble with tears in their eyes when they find the beaten, brutalized body of a small child. For my peace of mind, the thought of welcoming arms in a heavenly place seem to be the only salvation when I examine the body of a murdered child.

One of my duties is to care for that dead child's body. I must carry out my duties to document the crime that has been done both to the parents and to society at large. I must preserve and recognize the evidence so that one day someone might be brought to justice. I am often asked if I have become callous at performing death investigation and postmortem examinations, and I must respond in the following manner: If I am overcome with emotion and I forget my obligation when I have the opportunity to examine this child's body, in the years to come when I am called upon to give testimony and to explain the injuries for a jury making a decision, I would not have fulfilled my responsibilities as a medical examiner to that body. Professional detachment is a difficult concept for medical students, young physicians, law enforcement officers, and even attorneys to understand. The fact is that I only have one opportunity to preserve and document the horror of what has happened to a child and I cannot afford to let go of it. The moment I let go, I will be called upon to educate that decision-making body in the courtroom. It is the jury who decides a person's guilt or innocence, not the medical examiner. If I, in an emotional state, overlook a minute fact, I could be responsible for someone not being held accountable for the death of a child. Somehow I have to reach down and find another place in my heart to put this tragedy so that I might use intellect to help me document the demise of the child so his death will not have been in vain.

As we consider the emotional strength it takes to perform the postmortem examination of a murdered child we must also consider that, in today's society, no matter how horrific the killing of the child, rarely does our legal system hand down the same criminal justice penalties to an individual who is found guilty of murdering a child. The penalties of murdering an adult are much harsher and much longer. Sometimes I wonder what it is that allows society to choose the importance of one's life, no matter how short or how long their life span was. All I know is that at some point and time that child's purpose was not yet recognized or fulfilled in our society. His potential will never be reached and his productivity will never be measured. All the things that child could have become will never be realized. It sometimes grieves me when I look at the jury outcome in a child's homicide but I must remember that it is not my role to judge. Therefore, when I see a minimal penalty given in a child's death I must maintain the belief that if one escapes justice in this life, at some point in the unknown future he will be judged by a much higher power.

When Children Ask About Death

I can vividly recall listening to sermons in church as a child and hearing the preacher talking about damnation and threatening the congregation that if we did not join church that day, one of us might go outside, be hit by a car, and go straight to hell. That put a lot of fear into my young heart. At one point, I thought that people just joined church out of fear of death instead of love of God. The minister seemed to be contradicting the other lessons learned in church and Sunday school. I used to wonder if it was wrong to join church out of fear. We are supposed to believe in what the Bible says and the teachings of Jesus. As I grew older, I developed a theory that between heaven and hell was life on earth. I figured that if you tried to live right you have a better chance of going to heaven or wherever you consider heaven to be. As I grew up and developed my own personal sense of reason, and became more widely read, I realized that all preachers did not preach the way my childhood pastor did and there was nothing to fear from learning about God.

This brings me to the question I am often asked by adults: "Should I discuss the death of a relative with my child?" I say, "Yes." If the child asks you about death, then try to be as honest as you can. It is important for you to understand that children do encounter death in their daily lives. When you consider what is shown in cartoons and television programs, there are opportunities for the parent or the adult caretaker to discuss death with a young person. As I recall my own childhood, not only was I exposed to the concept of death from church but also I recall the concept of death in the cartoons. I remember asking my mother what R.I.P.

meant on a tombstone when the figure of a cartoon character being shot, burned up, or rolled over by a steamroller was shown.

Of course children think about death but they do not necessarily dwell on it, nor should they. In today's world there is so much information about the death and dying process that it does seep into children's programs. When asked about how to tell a child about death, I can only respond in this simple way: Be honest when the question is asked and consider the age or maturity of your child. You have to consider the relationship of the deceased to the child. The child may ask, "What happened to Grandma and Grandpa?" If the adult says, "I do not know," then the child may wonder for a long time and internalize the questions. When it is a parent who dies and a very young child is told that Mommy or Daddy is not coming back, make sure that it is followed with a discussion when that child is older about how the parent died. You should also explain that the death was not the child's fault. It is important to gently discuss the death of a young sibling as well. There are too many children who become disturbed and feel that they have been the cause of a person's death. Often many adults will tell a young child that the person died because it was God's plan, or God's will. I suggest that perhaps you talk with your religious leader or family physician. I would hate to have a child grow up thinking that God is evil and mean and that He just decided to take away a loved one. It is often more simple and honest for the adult to say to the child, "I do not know why our relative got sick."

I feel that it is healthy if the parent has the opportunity to discuss the concept of death with a child in a calm and simple fashion. Using examples of family pets can be helpful. If you are driving down a road and see a dead animal and a child asks about it, that also is an opportunity for a discussion. Conversations about death do, again, depend on the child's age and level of understanding.

Sadly, some children find out from strangers, that they had lost a parent or sibling when they were infants. Sometimes this news is harmful. There are going to be times in a child's life when he will encounter a classmate who becomes ill and dies, or dies traumatically in a fire or motor vehicle accident. The child may have questions and, again, I urge the caretaker to consult a physician or religious leader for guidance. There are also plenty of articles, magazines, and books on the subject of how to explain death to a child. The point that I want to emphasize is that children are aware of death. It is the adult participation and, perhaps, what they read or are exposed to, that sets the reality guideline and separates make-believe from the world in which we live.

Another aspect of a child dealing with death is the amount of violence that children are exposed to on a regular basis. It may be that our teenagers appear to be preoccupied with death. Part of this could be a dependence on the media, which portrays death as a solution for social problems. It is important that adults maintain a monitoring force of what young people are exposed to. There is an abundance of violence and death portrayed in the more popular computer games, and in some of the gruesome toys that are on the market. It is important that our children remain involved with healthy play and imagination. In other words, it is important for the adult to be involved with the child in play as well as in relaxation. Adults are here to be involved with the lives of children and to keep them entertained and use opportunities to teach them. The same thing can be said for some of our programming on television. If you think a child knows nothing about death, sit with him and watch the programming that is on during the "family hour."

In the forensic pathology arena, healthcare providers carefully assess the level of maturity of a child at the age of ten or eleven. Most psychologists feel that a child around this age knows right from wrong and can begin to deal with the concepts of life and death. There comes a time when there is an appropriate opportunity to discuss death in a healthier way. Sometimes you cannot avoid the subject when a loved one dies. If your child asks a question about death, above all, try to be honest. After all, you are the adult person in that young one's life. He is looking up to you and he expects and deserves some honesty. We all know that parenting does not come with how-to tags, so I suggest that you seek some guidance from a trained professional. I was very fortunate to have been able to change my concept of death from fear outside of church to real consequences of life. There are so many things in the world that cause fear in children, as well as adults. Now is the time to have those discussions.

  The acts of terrorism that have stricken the nerves of this country have also penetrated into the psyche of our young people. Not only are they exposed to repetitive news commentary and periodicals, the concept of fear and uncertainty can be very persuasive. Children are seeking a level of comfort and adults must continue to provide that for them. Since September 11, 2001, children are asking about death more frequently and exhibiting fear of strangers, flying and traumatic injuries. Death is a difficult topic for adults to talk about so I certainly understand trepidation of parents having to discuss dying with a child. I wish you much luck and, remember, honesty is the best policy.

When Life Becomes Too Painful

Suicides are some of the most difficult investigations for a medical examiner to conduct due to the social stigma attached to these deaths. They are also some of the most painful cases to explain to the survivors, who are often left looking for answers. It is a shame that there remains such a high stigma to suicide in this country's general population. The same can be said for the response of insurance companies when a loved one has committed suicide. The problem is knowing that the family or the loved one's friends will have questions about what could have been done to prevent the tragedy. Unfortunately, there are no answers. For every case I have investigated where there were signs of suicide, there are an additional four cases where there is absolutely no clue or indication that the event was about to occur. The surviving family remains tormented. It is a myth that people who commit suicide always leave notes. In fact, it is rare that a note is found. I have come to the conclusion there are certain individuals who, once they decide to terminate their own life, will go to any length to do so.

I have, through my years of experience, developed a discussion for classifying certain categories of suicides. The first category of people more likely to commit suicide are the elderly, the last person living in his family, or lonely people who feel that they have lost contact with their immediate family. In many situations, these individuals have suffered chronic, debilitating diseases and feel they are burdens to their family. They have lost the will and desire to live. Many of these individuals will use guns or hang themselves in order to end their lives. Others will amass a large number of prescription pills and take them all at once. It is heartbreaking to investigate a death like this. Often these people have lived alone for long periods of time, without visitors, and their bodies are found many days or weeks after death has occurred. I do not condone the taking of one's life, but I wonder about these unfortunate individuals and the quality of life they have lived. I have a sense of understanding of the pain they were in.

The next category of suicide victims are those who, because of chronic disease, life-changing illness or injury, or circumstance, will take their own lives. These individuals have often suffered traumatic injuries and can no longer be the person they were. They may be confined to a wheelchair, not have the use of their limbs or, in some way, have become unable to care for themselves. Somehow they have suffered a tremendous life change and they cannot cope with these new circumstances. Oftentimes, they cannot stand the fact that someone has to take care of them. Many times when investigators evaluate the history of these individuals as told by their caretakers, one can almost visualize when the idea of suicide came to mind. The person's personality changes. There might remain a lot of anger about what happened to transform the person's life.

Many of these individuals are suffering with chronic pain. Some have developed an addiction to prescription pain medications. Many have had such an abrupt change in their life, they remain unhappy. Thus, they end their lives, often with prescription drugs or by violence such as a self-inflicted wound. Many leave a note thanking their caretaker and apologizing to their family, saying that they are better off dead. The surviving loved ones are often overcome with pain and guilt, thinking they have done something wrong. It takes a long time for these survivors to come to the understanding that there was nothing they could have done to prevent the suicide. Was the death right or wrong? All I can say is that it is between the decedent and God. These surviving family members and friends need counseling to understand that they did nothing wrong.

A third category of suicide victims is young adults and children. In this category the person or people have ended their lives as a result of something they perceived as being the main reason they were living. Many times it is a broken romance, but it can also be the loss of a job, humiliation, or even fear. It is particularly unfortunate that young people do not have the necessary coping skills to deal with a broken relationship or the disappointment of bad grades. In all the cases I have observed while reconstructing the life of a suicide victim, it becomes clear that the victim's self-esteem was so low any little thing that changed in his life could have pushed him over the edge. These changes would not affect most people who have coping abilities or have had prior experience or adult figures that they could look to for strength. Most of these issues could have been dealt with and taken in equal stride. For some reason, these unfortunate individuals could not look beyond the problem.

These people are more prone to take their lives by violent means, whether it be by the use of a firearm, hanging, or something as dramatic as throwing themselves off a rooftop. Their deaths are usually rapid and completely unpredictable. Again, the loved ones are left wondering why they did not recognize the signs. I say to these survivors, again and again, that it would be difficult to have predicted this outcome. Many things that we take for granted have extremely harsh effects on those individuals without well-formed coping skills. These individuals cannot look past their traumatic experience and imagine what life would be like on the other side.

It is hard to imagine a ten-year-old killing herself over poor body image, but it happens. It is difficult to imagine a thirteen-year-old killing himself over a broken relationship, but it happens. I can go on and on with examples, but you get the point. The families are left to wonder why, and these survivors need a lot of aftercare. The victims' friends and family are often permanently traumatized, particularly when the victim was very young. The surviving family and friends assume blame and feel responsible for the individual's death. It is so very difficult for these survivors. These younger victims will often leave a note or an indication of their suicide by some other mechanism, whether it is a record or a computer image, or something as drastic as a message written in their blood.   Most of the time the victims indicate in their message that there was something wrong with them and the world is better off without their presence. What a tragedy!

There are other types of deaths that are determined to be suicide from the investigation of the scene and the reconstructing of events. Many of these cases are ruled as such because of the individual's participation and the behavior that led to the person's death. Some of these cases involve people who play with guns. This is where the medical examiner's ruling becomes very difficult.

It is a general concept that an adult who picks up a gun and pulls the trigger has played a role in his own death. The most common example I can give is someone who chooses to play Russian roulette. That person is handling an instrument that has a known dangerous or fatal outcome. He places the weapon against his head and pulls the trigger. By his action and participation in this event, he has caused his own death. The same holds true for a person who uses a starting pistol, even though it does not have a bullet. A starting pistol has gunpowder, and the firing of this gun, applied closely to the body, may result in fatal damage. This has been reported in the media and has happened in Hollywood. What the medical examiner has to investigate and determine is how emotionally developed the person was, how the particular weapon operated, and whether the weapon could actually discharge itself.

Some of the most challenged cases are those of an apparent contact gunshot wound on a decedent who is found surrounded by materials used to clean guns. The family may argue that the deceased was cleaning a gun and it accidentally went off. Usually what is found on the body is a contact gunshot wound where the gun was held tightly against the body. Forensic pathologists usually find defects in the head or the chest indicating that the muzzle was held against the body as the gun was fired. What a pathologist must explain to the family is a person's intent is not being judged but rather the outcome of the person's action. These cases deserve full investigation with swabbing of the hands to help determine whether there is gunshot residue from firing the weapon. These are very difficult cases to investigate and very difficult rulings for families to accept. Every case must be judged on an individual basis.

In dealing with children with self-inflicted gunshot wounds, it is important to establish not only the chronological age but also the emotional age of the child. In medicine, physicians consider above ten or eleven as the average age of reason. It is felt that a child older than this should know the difference between right and wrong and should have some basic knowledge about gun safety. It is difficult to do this assessment and a lot depends on establishing the level of the emotional development and maturity of the individual child. These cases result in conflicts within families when it is unknown how the child was able to get hold of a gun, and whether or not the concept of gun safety had been practiced within that household. It is extremely sad when these deaths occur because a young child was probably imitating what he had seen on television or at the movies. This type of self-inflicted death happens all too frequently in this country. There is a tremendous need for gun-safety education, not only in the home by the family but also by various forms of media. I feel that every program on television that shows someone committing suicide has a responsibility to end that show with information on mental health and gun safety.

When a child is found to be under the age of reason either by chronological or emotional development, then the shooting is ruled an accident. Even when a minor picks up a gun, points, and shoots it at another person this action is considered an accident based upon the child's lack of maturity in recognizing right and wrong. I can only imagine the heartbreak that accompanies these cases.

In the matter of playing with guns I must share my opinion: I realize that every child who plays with a toy gun is not going to shoot himself. I recall playing with toy guns as a child. But, I also recall being taught about guns and being shown the difference between reality and a toy. Unfortunately, today there are too many deaths of toddlers because of what they have seen somebody else do. I believe in gun safety and I certainly hope that at some point, our community will realize that increased safety standards will ensure safety for our children.

There is another unfortunate part of investigating a self-inflicted wound that leads to death. Many families are jolted to reality when they realize their insurance company is not going to pay a policy when there has been a medical determination of suicide. Unfortunately, many people are not aware of the insurance protocol, and have not read the fine print when signing their policies. There are insurance policies that contain clauses that state that if an individual was found to have consumed alcohol, tobacco, or a drug which was determined to have played a role in the person's death, the beneficiaries may not be paid the policy premium. Many families need to know that if a person has committed suicide within two years of taking out a life insurance policy, it is doubtful that the benefits will be paid. It is extremely unfortunate when families call me to say they have spent tremendous amounts of money on a funeral service and realized too late that the insurance policy would not be paid because of the circumstances related to the individual's death. On top of lacking insurance benefits, the families are grieving and need answers, but sometimes those answers are not available.

From my standpoint, many suicide victims have been in need of counseling or other forms of treatment prior to their death. Perhaps the one thing we can do in this country is to continue to educate the public that being depressed, sad, or not in control of your emotions does not mean that you are weak. It may mean that you need to talk with somebody or you need someone to listen. We all need somebody at some time. Those in need of support should never feel ashamed about their mental-health adjustments. This discussion on suicide is not meant to be totally inclusive of all the cases that I investigate but, hopefully, to give strength to some families who are looking for answers. To those reading this who have had a close friend or relative who has taken his own life, I hope you find comfort in the knowledge that maybe the person is in a better place. There are support groups in your community to help you cope with your loss.

If there are questions surrounding you loved one's death that remain unanswered, it may be beneficial to have a meeting with your local medical examiner to understand how the doctor reached his conclusions.

When Reality Hits Home

The worst fears of many Americans occurred on September 11, 2001, when the seemingly impossible happened. The terrorist attacks on the World Trade Center, the Pentagon, and the crash in Pennsylvania struck the very core of this country's nerve. The freedom that had been so carelessly tossed about before was jerked into consciousness of all who were old enough to watch the television screens on that fateful day.

As a child, I recall learning in American and world history classes about how the United States had never suffered an attack on the continent. With the exception of the bombing of Pearl Harbor, this country had remained relatively untouched by acts of war and terrorism that occurred regularly in other parts of the world. As I remember the passages, the text seemed to gloat that no such attack would ever happen within our borders. But a new chapter in our American history has been written.

How do we deal with the manmade disaster that has occurred? It is virtually impossible to act as though nothing has changed. American citizens have had a rude awakening to the fact that no one is safe from terrorist activities, even within our society. It is important that we feel secure, whether it be at home, school, work, or socially. It should be recognized that a certain segment of our society will use this tragedy as an excuse to live without regard to the future and there will be a measurable increase in recreational drug use, perhaps the spread of sexually transmitted diseases, or rethinking of plans leading to reckless personal behavior. We are already experiencing a change in the American travel habits as well as general consumer spending.

It strikes me as odd that the bombing of the Oklahoma federal building was not recognized as a call to update our national security systems on all levels. In many people's minds, it was an isolated incident, or was that wishful thinking? Perhaps we wanted to ignore the fact that an American citizen would kill innocent people as a vendetta against our government. Instead of a call to action, the anniversary of that horrible tragedy is mourned annually by a small group of survivors and their families and carefully observed by a handful of federal agencies.

Likewise, the rising number of fatal school shootings by disgruntled teenagers has led this country to the perplexing conundrum of being unable to develop a characteristic description of who could carry out such dastardly deeds. In its place is a continuous abandonment of a troubled national public school system and failure to address the issues behind school violence.

The recurrent issues of racial strife evidenced by the increasing number of blacks and Hispanics who die in police custody, inhabit our jails and prisons, and who are the constant recipients of the disparities in healthcare education and the ability to achieve the American dream of home ownership, continue to result in one of the highest national homicide rates of the industrial free world. These same issues affect those who live in poverty with a similar frequency, no matter what their ethnic background.

The result of all these situations has been escalating violence and tragic deaths that have left individuals, groups, and now a nation, to cope with unexplainable and incomprehensible losses of life. Not only are the family members and friends grieving, but also the way in which the world communicates allows others to experience the profound effects of real-time coverage of violent deaths.

The long-term effect of the continuous media coverage on the human psyche has yet to be determined. One can imagine the fear that may have plagued the citizens of this country when the bombing of Pearl Harbor occurred or as the Allied Forces advanced in Europe. The current daily carnage of civil strife in Central America and African nations has long been relegated to the international sections of the newspapers unless the event was found to be newsworthy to the general American public. For the most part, these acts of senseless violence happened in other places and could not have been imagined to one day be in our own backyards. Until now most Americans have denied that such an event like the attacks on America could have happened.

Now, the country is not only dealing with the relatively small retraction of personal freedoms but with the images and fears of a massive loss of life and residual images of September 11, 2001. Images of human bodies being strewn from the imploding World Trade Towers and vivid descriptions of fragmented body parts have been etched into the minds of hundreds of thousands of citizens, along with the recurrent thought of this type of tragedy occurring again. The fear of flying commercial airliners is sure to be a long-term reminder of the effects of the terrorist campaign.

The shock of seeing a real human body dismembered or severely deformed is unlike anything that a horror film can portray. When we go to the movies our subconscious copes with the terror by reminding us that what we are seeing is

not real. The depictions of human suffering on the

news from the September 11 tragedy were almost

surreal and left most people in a state of shock and

denial. The bystanders and survivors not only have

had to deal with the memories of lost loved ones

and colleagues but with the feeling that there is no

physical way to say good-bye to many of the

victims of that attack.

It has been the practice of the culture in this

country to publicly grieve as we lay our dead to

rest. No matter what the time span between death

and the final interment, Americans have

participated in these rituals, usually with the dead

persons' body having been viewed by next of kin

prior to services. Although not law, the practice of

enduring a wake is commonplace. Even when the

human body has been badly decomposed, the

surviving friends and family have found some solace with which to begin the grieving process. They have been given information that the postmortem examination has conclusively determined that the remains are those of their loved one. Even though a body may not be present at the funeral, science can assist the family by assuring them that their loved ones' body is in a safe place and that it can be laid to rest in a proper fashion. Due to the thoroughness of the postmortem examination, it is possible to identify a person through scars, tattoos, previous surgery sites, and other unique physical means that can provide identifying and calming information to the next of kin. Hopefully, the results of the science of forensic anthropology and DNA identification technology can be helpful in bringing some closure to families. Even with the identification proven via DNA it will undoubtedly take some time for acceptance of the death to penetrate the heart and mind of a grieving person.

It is usually my recommendation that family and friends not view the remains when there has been extensive decomposition or disfiguring injuries. Many families will demand to see their loved one's body but then they cannot get that image out of their minds. It is best to find a scar or identifying marking such as a birthmark and photograph only that part of the body. Family members can view the picture without exposing the relatives to the condition of the corpse.

The problem that occurs when the human body is virtually destroyed during injury or prolonged postmortem period is that it is more difficult for the survivors to accept the death as having happened and the finality that one will never see his loved one again.

Acceptance has always been problematic in deaths that have consumed the human body such as fires, airplane crashes, and explosions. The most common response when we learn of a loved one's sudden or violent death is one of disbelief, so when a person perishes in an explosion their relatives may be in denial. The most common flow of the human grief reaction has been described as shock, denial, anger, and then acceptance. Of course this order does not hold true for everyone. It stands to reason that if the human mind has the innate inability to contemplate its own demise that the untimely demise of someone close to you may be equally as difficult to grasp.

Even when informed in a sensitive way of the disaster, loved ones experience the thought that unless they are shown their relatives' body there remains a small hope that the person is not dead. This is natural. It takes time for an individual to face the sad fact that the person being grieved is gone. To understand this phenomenon, think back to images of medial portrayals of a person lost at sea. How many times have we watched movies and television shows that have a person reappearing after many years when he has been declared dead? Suddenly, the character is back and the grieving family must readjust to the changes. That is what we all want to expect when someone we love is suddenly taken from us. Only time will tell how the individual and society as a whole deal with the events of September 11. Because only time, patience, and understanding will begin to heal some of the wounds created from the massive loss of life, as well as personal and national security.

One thing that has become clear in the aftermath is that those who counsel the bereaved often have not experienced the personal or professional exposure to the destruction of the human body. It became clear that those challenged with this great responsibility needed more constructive training in recognizing their personal responses to death before they could offer help to others. This is a role that is often overlooked when disaster planning is taking place. I continue to encourage emergency units, public safety officers, and clergy to take part in learning how to understand the finality of death.

For the families who are unable to say good-bye in the traditional way, I encourage a spiritual route. It is important that you understand the scientific procedures that are being used for identification and what the limitations are. Despite the advances of DNA use in forensics, every fragment of human tissue cannot be identified. As much as possible the family must be informed of the process and problems with identification. This is very important when the media is involved. Control must be exercised to make sure that the affected families are made aware of positive identification before the media broadcasts on the evening news or in the daily papers.

When there are problems in identifying human remains or the remains are co-mingled, I try to involve the family or their chosen representatives in the process. I have worked on cases where upon conclusion of the recovery effort there was a residual mass of human flesh that was impossible to identify. I informed the next of kin and allowed them to share in the decision of whether to perform a mass burial or to accept a portion of the unidentified tissue for a memorial service. At least the family feels as though they were considered in the decision-making process.

I have had many reporters and law-enforcement agents tell me that they became a believer in God or had a spiritual awakening when they started doing human recovery work. I thank God for my compassion when I need to assist the grieving family through the process. When you cannot say good-bye physically, the spiritual aspect can be helpful. My heart breaks for those who struggle to understand the death of a loved one and are unable to go through the grieving process due to the destruction of the human body. I can only continue to keep them in my prayers and give them the time and distance they require to cope with the loss of that special someone.

God bless our nation as we struggle to understand.

Bitter Medicine

Traditional medical education in this country is usually comprised of two major segments. The first part of medical school is known as preclinical science, where students build upon the foundation of chemistry and biology and knowing how the body works through understanding of these basic sciences. Preclinical is usually taken during the first two years of medical school. During the second year students are preparing for patient interaction along with understanding the physiology of bodily function. The third and fourth years of medical school are known as the clinical years where students apply their knowledge of basic science with hands-on approach to patient care.

The third-year medical student is assigned to a team for purposes of patient care and education. These medical teams are made up of multiple layers. First you have the head of the team, known as the attending physician, who is considered the supreme being in the hospital setting, at least in the mind of the medical student. The attending doctor basically has all authority over your future medical career. The next component in the team is the senior residents who are just about to finish their postgraduate training. Then there are the junior residents who may be one or two years out of medical school and are just beginning to feel that they have accomplished quite a bit. The next level is composed of the intern or the immediate postgraduate medical student. The interns are always trying to make sure that they did the right thing and stay out of everybody's way, especially the attending physician. The lowest level on the medical team is the student. We always felt, as lowly medical students, that it was our job to do all the dirty things that no other physician wanted to do, like taking specimens to the lab and administering laxatives. The team approach to medicine is unique and very important to understanding the growth of medical knowledge and development of confidence to interact with patients and gain information about them.

As a medical student, I closely observed what was being taught to me, frequently around the bedside or in the hallways of the hospitals. There was a lot of information gained about diagnosing, treating, curing and preventing disease. I never heard about the death process. I do not recall having one lecture in medical school that prepared us, as students, for what to do when a patient dies. There are no instructions given on how to inform the family. The situation was never dealt with. I would always think *if we are learning medicine, aren't we supposed to be able to deal with death as well?* When I would ask the attending physicians or the doctor senior to me about death the answer was always the same: "This is a health-care institution. This is a place concerned with life. Our job is to prevent death." I could never agree with that. It had always been my thought that death was a part of life. Having witnessed so many chronically ill people with no chance of recovering from their diseases I felt that in many cases death could be merciful.

I recall one day observing an intern struggling after one of the patients on our service had died. He had been told simply to call the family and give notification. He had also been told to notify the medical examiner's office. This young doctor did not know what to say to either party. He did not know why he was calling the medical examiner's office. He did not know what words to use with the family. He had agony etched on his face and I felt badly for him. I wondered, *what could he say.* I did not think that he knew the family because they had primarily dealt with the attending physician. This was a teaching hospital, after all, and the attending physician was the head of the team and responsible for the patient's care. Here the intern was about to make a death notification and he was uncomfortable and unfamiliar with a family who soon would be grieving. I took the opportunity to approach him and simply said to him, "Whatever you say, introduce yourself, ask them if this is a good time to talk with them, and let them know you have some bad news. Make sure you pause and ask them if they need to sit down." I told him not to just blurt the information out because that would hurt, but to try to be gentle. I know this doctor was stunned by what I said, but I think that he took it in stride. I watched him make the call from the nursing desk and, being a few feet away, I could hear the screams coming through the phone. The intern just became ashen as he stumbled through his ill-prepared speech. The family screamed that they were coming to the hospital right away and he mumbled something and hung up. This doctor looked mortified, but I think he had learned something. I know I did. I learned at least that I could be honest, direct, and sensitive to an unknown person on the other end of the phone.

I have never believed that death was not an issue for physicians to be concerned about. If a doctor cannot deal with death then how do we expect a family to deal with it? I believe that our medical education fails young physicians in this area, even today. Death is part of the cycle of life. From my point of view, death happens to all of us. Yes, it is the great unknown but it does happen, and it will always happen.

Many physicians will call me and say with great emotion that their patient should not have died. I have to remind these physicians, gently, that death is not in the doctor's control. Some deaths are not preventable. No matter what we as physicians do with the healing art, death has a way of occurring. No matter how advanced we are scientifically, death is not always ours to control.

If we began to teach medical students and physicians to deal with the issue of death, the community would be much better off. So many times physicians miss an opportunity to be honest with patients and families. There is no pleasant way to inform someone that their loved one has died, even if they are standing at the bedside and there are

DNR (do not resuscitate) instructions. Part of the

medical-school curriculum needs to be modified to

discuss with young physicians how they should

approach families. You may never know the

precise words for every occasion, but there is a way

to put the death announcement in more personal

terms. To be able to calmly discuss a patient's

death or impending death with the family may save

a whole lot of terror for both the loved ones and the

physicians.

Too often, forensic pathologists are invited

to lecture to medical students, almost as a form of

entertainment. I find nothing entertaining about

looking at slides depicting violent or gory deaths. A

golden opportunity is missed to let medical students

know that conversing about death is difficult. The

medical examiner or forensic pathologist should be

better utilized to help familiarize medical students and physicians with the death process. After all, death investigation is our chosen medical specialty and who best to talk about end of life issues? I resist the temptation to shock students and to tell them gory stories. I want to make sure that young physicians are aware that the cadaver lying in the anatomy lab is the body of somebody's loved one. To make it more personal I ask them to close their eyes and imagine the person that they love the most in this position. Then I say, "Ask yourself, would you want your loved one's body laughed at or would you want it handled with sensitivity and maturity?" Physicians have an obligation. It does not have to be bitter medicine. Medical examiners, forensic pathologists, and clinicians can work together. We must all realize that life and death are part of the same spectrum. We must learn to take our own bitter medicine.

Forensic Pathology Is More Than Shock Value

Most hospital physicians cannot explain what a medical examiner actually does. Hospital physicians often share the same fear of death that laypeople do. Many times a medical examiner is used as a weapon to convince families to have autopsies performed in a hospital setting. In the hospital, where there are pathology departments, the patient who dies of natural causes may be examined in that facility. In that setting the family has a choice to say yes or no to having an autopsy performed and the ability to limit how much of the body will be examined by the pathologist. In the hospital setting the autopsy is performed to determine a natural cause of death or to evaluate whether the diagnosis or treatment was helpful.

The forensic pathologist, of course, performs autopsies in a non-hospital setting under local laws where there is no consent required from families. The autopsy in a forensic setting is done under the public law with the need to know why people die. Although a consent process is not used, medical examiners do try to work with families to allay their fears about what is going to happen to their loved one's body while in the custody of the government.

Unfortunately, the exposure of impressionable students to the specialty of forensic pathology is very limited. A medical examiner or forensic pathologist is usually asked to come and give a one-or two-hour lecture to the second-year medical students. This has come to be known as Shock Theater because many of the tools used to teach about forensic pathology are pictures, usually, of violent deaths. Forensic pathology is a lot more than just a one or two hour shock lecture. This is an opportunity to introduce medical students to a possible career choice. It is a chance to orient the medical student to the subject of death and dealing with the surviving family and the legal issues that surround a patient's death. This is an opportunity to draw on the experience of the young student in examining the cycle of life, disease, injury, and death. There are opportunities that are missed because the medical examiner is not utilized fully in the teaching of medical students. What I have observed in the last several years are mandates of medical students to observe at least one autopsy before they graduate. Oftentimes that is literally the day before graduation.

Because there is not enough orientation to the death process or the function of a medical examiner's office, hospitals are usually at a loss when discussing death with survivors. When a medical diagnosis has not been made due to a short or emergent hospitalization, that deceased individual will need to have an autopsy conducted to determine what happened. Many times I am contacted by irate family members or perturbed hospital staff who have been in curt discussions with one another over the proposed autopsy of a deceased person. I try to encourage the hospital staff to take a slower approach in asking consent for hospital autopsies, or to consult with me, or my pathology staff, prior to discussing this. Frequently hospital physicians will ask for an autopsy to be performed purely for academic reasons. It is almost a-waste of professional energy when an individual with a known chronic disease, which has been diagnosed and treated for several months or years, is sent to the medical examiner's office for autopsy. I am aware that there have been instances where the family is told that they have no choice and an autopsy will be done. Often those cases arrive at the medical examiner's office, but because there is a qualified medical history, no autopsy will be performed. It would be very helpful if hospital staffs were more aware of the types of examinations that are performed by forensic pathologists in the medical examiner's office. Due to limited staff and budgets, not all decedents with medical history will undergo an autopsy.

It is beneficial for families to understand the process of death investigation and why it has to take place, particularly when there is reluctance to allow an autopsy to be performed on a relative's body. The autopsy has great benefit for the family to gain an understanding of the cause of death, as well as for the treating physician to take what has been learned from the deceased and extend it to others in hopes that they might live longer lives. The tenseness associated with the autopsy being performed in a hospital could be alleviated if the physician and other medical staff felt more comfortable in explaining the autopsy to families and the role of medical examiners. In other words, the medical examiner should be utilized just a little bit more than just for one or two lectures to young medical students. While there are only a few forensic pathologists as compared to internal medical specialists, pediatricians, and surgeons, medical examiners do fulfill a necessary role. I think, perhaps, if there were more partnership and collaboration between the clinical physicians and medical examiners, there would be fewer allegations of malpractice and more relieved medical staff and family members.

The Art Of The Autopsy

The human being is the most fascinating animal living on Earth today. Our bodies are works of art. Our unique joints, upright posture, anatomy, as well as our minds set us apart from lower animals. As a physician and scientist, I am constantly fascinated by the individual characteristics of our bodies. I cannot fathom how anyone can feel that the human body just evolved without divine intervention.

Since I cannot talk to my patients I must do the most thorough examination that I can. I must immerse myself in a particular person's story, history, and circumstances of death, as well as, closely study his body. There is a story to be told by examining human remains. I do not mean to sound ghoulish. I want the reader to understand that careful observation with an open mind will gain and provide so much information. The human body does speak to me, and then I, in turn, speak on its behalf.

I believe in a total postmortem examination. Even little things like the condition of the toenails, such as their texture, thickness, length, and color may tell me a lot about the deceased person's circulation and hygiene. The skin on the soles of the feet is important to consider, whether it is soft or hard. Sometimes examining a foot can tell me about the shoes that the person wore. The skeletal structure can tell me about a person's posture. There may have been habitual stooping, indicating lack of self-esteem. The body shape can tell me how well a person ate. Muscular development can tell me about a person's strength, nutritional status, and exercise habits. All of these things come from being an observer of the human form. In addition, I can tell about a person's habits, such as the amount of sun exposure, which lead to liver spots on the extremities, excessive tan lines, or even premature wrinkling. It may sound bizarre, but on occasion I analyze the contents of the belly button. These observations tell me something about what that person did and how he took care of himself. Many times it may not add to the information that I am gathering to tell me how the person died, but it adds to telling me how he lived.

Often the medical examiner becomes a voyeur into the deceased person's lifestyle and life choices. It is not, in my view, professional to expose many of the things that I have witnessed during my career as a death investigator. The point that I am making is that as a medical examiner I cannot afford to be judgmental. The medical examiner must have an open mind and simply document facts. There have been numerous cases

where I have observed a properly dressed

individual, male or female, only to find upon

undressing the body that the individual was clad in

unusual undergarments. There are also times that I

observe that a body has been dressed by another

individual after death, just by noticing how the

clothes are arranged. There are other things about

the human body that gives me insight into personal

habits. I notice whether body hair is present,

shaved, or recently shaved. I observe the presence

of scars, their age, the way that they are placed, and

their state of healing. Many telltale signs are

revealed by close examination of the hands and

fingernails. It is important for me to look at the

arms and neck when I suspect a suicidal injury. It

should not surprise the reader to learn that more

than one body has been brought in as a designated

sex but upon close inspection, revealed to be the opposite sex. Medical examiners must uphold the law and consider medical ethics. If an individual has gone through a sex change, the person remains the sex he has chosen to become. Even if the person is genetically male and lives as a female, he remains female. Medical examiners speak for the dead and often keep their secrets.

The shape and contour of the body can provide additional information to the death investigator. Not only can we determine the state of nutrition and the amount of exercise, there are often times that we make a determination that we are examining the body of a habitual smoker. Sometimes the body reveals to us if the characteristics have been recently changed such as shaving or dyeing of the hair, or the attachment of hairpieces. The shape of the head, the condition of the facial skin, the presence or absence of teeth, and the condition of the gums reveal a lot about habits and health of the decedent. There is so much to be gained by close observation and this is only the beginning of the examination.

The overall condition of the human body at death must be carefully assessed. This is when I must lay on hands. In other words, I have got to touch the body. It is not enough to look at the body to make the assessment; I ensure that assessment is correct through touching. I can get a feel for the condition of the skin, the degree of moisture, or evidence of malnutrition. Because I am a firm believer that many of our diseases are rooted in poor nutritional habits I make it my business to do a full assessment of the condition of the body so that I may relay my discovery to the family or treating physician. The pathologist cannot stand across the room and simply look. You must touch. This is where my learning, education, and experiences are called into play. As simple as it seems, it would be wrong for me to just stand and look. There are numerous conditions that I can detect by touching a dead person's body. There are fine delicate scars that I feel by running my fingers over the skin.

It is irritating to me when I see a medical examiner portrayed on television who is asked to determine when a person died. The fictitious character is often seen striding across the room spending five seconds with the body and then coming back and saying that the decedent had been dead for two hours and twenty-two minutes. This is an extreme disservice to real medical examiners and forensic scientists who touch the body. Medical examiners have to apply science, medical knowledge, and common sense to try to make a determination as to the range of time when an individual has died.

There are three conditions that must be assessed primarily at the scene that guide pathologists in determining when a person has died. I must say that medical examiners are making an educated guess. It takes a little more than five seconds of touching the body to determine a range as to when a person may have died. The only time that we can be exact is if there is an eyewitness or something catastrophic occurs at a particular place and time, like a witness to an explosion who gives a statement to the public that the blast sounded at the start of the eleven o'clock news.

The conditions that we assess are as follows: rigor mortis, livor mortis, and algor mortis. These assessments are made within the first twenty-four hours, if possible.

Rigor mortis is the stiffening of the body that occurs within the first forty-eight hours of death. It develops from a buildup of lactic acid in the muscular tissue. Rigor mortis is caused by anaerobic (absence of oxygen) functioning of muscular tissue which can function for a short period without oxygen. Rigor is the cause of the myth that leads to the old wife's tale that bodies move after death. It is a scientific phenomenon that the joints will move, particularly in the arms and fingers. Rigor mortis develops from the head downward within the first two hours of death. It is usually fully formed within twenty-four hours. It becomes complete in twenty-four hours to thirty-six hours and then begins to disappear after that time. It is accelerated when the person has been physically active right before death or under conditions of heat or fever. Rigor mortis is often observed at autopsy. Because of the muscular structure, rigor mortis is usually limited in the very young and the very old because of the different amounts of muscle tissue development.

Livor mortis is the pooling of blood in the body, which is associated with gravity. It is often observed two to four hours after death. Usually presented as a pink to purple discoloration, depending on the person's level of pigmentation, livor mortis can also be related to a person's level of anemia or amount of residual blood in the body. Basically, blood will pool wherever a body has lain in a position for at least six hours. Livor mortis development makes the examiner aware many times that the body has been moved after death. It can be difficult to perceive in a person who is dark skinned but there are technical ways to evaluate it. Livor mortis may also be confused with bruises or abrasions. There are also technical ways to evaluate this through making a thin incision in the skin.

Many times death investigators come across cases where there is inappropriate livor mortis indicating that the body has been moved by individuals who have found the body and have tried to arouse the individual, not realizing he is dead.

Algor mortis is the rate of cooling of the human body. This is a very imprecise way to determine how long a person has been dead. Algor mortis is dependent on several variables that fluctuate around the country. The investigator has to consider a person's size, as a heavier person will cool at a slower rate than a thin person. The climate, humidity, and placement of the body and clothing also have to be considered as does whether the body is found indoors or outdoors, under air conditioning or humid, hot conditions. Algor mortis is measured by a thermometer either orally, in the underarm area, rectum, or even through piercing of the liver. It is a difficult assessment to make and must be used in conjunction with the other two early postmortem changes. The longer the postmortem period the less information the assessment of algor mortis yields.

All of these changes must be considered along with the investigative information developed about the deceased and the evaluation of the scene or place of death. There is nothing magic about death investigation. It is a collaborative effort with law enforcement, forensic investigators, proper training, and good judgment. I remain concerned that many individuals who sit on juries or judges all too often think the medical examiner should do exactly what Quincy did. This could be problematic. The bottom line in all of this is that in

order to obtain answers from the human body, to
learn from an examination of the person who has
died, pathologists have to take a real interest in that
body at that time.

The medical examiner, in order to be
successful in his investigation and examination,
must feel like the deceased he is examining is his
patient. A good examination is the last thing that a
medical examiner can do for the decedent. This is
how we tell a person's story. We must tell the story
with no bias, with a thorough examination,
excellent medical technique, and good common
sense. We must tell the dead person's story and
document it so that it will last and stand up to
questioning and scrutiny. We also want to help the
family and jury to understand what caused a
person's demise. We must tell the story in a way
that information can be shared and taken back to the

public to allow them to live longer, healthier lives based upon what we have learned from the dead. There is a tremendous benefit to doing a thorough examination of a dead body.

It is important to understand that the postmortem examination cannot be performed in a vacuum. When I say vacuum, I mean just the physician and the dead body. It is imperative that as much information as possible has been collected for review prior to beginning the examination. I always state that the scene and the autopsy are closely related. In my view, the autopsy actually begins at the scene where the body is found. Once that body is disturbed or moved from the site of death many variables become added to the equation. It is important that the medical examiner be able to review information furnished by investigators or police which will add some insight into the decedent's personal, and social habits, medical history, home life, and other conditions that will allow the medical examiner to arrive at reasonable conclusions as to the cause of a person's demise.

Due to the magnitude of investigations that must be carried out, most medical examiners employ trained death investigators to act as their eyes and ears at the scene of death. No matter what type of death is being investigated there is a need to collect a lot of facts. Whether the death is due to an automobile accident, use of a designer drug, or domestic violence, there is a need to gather information. It is important for a person to understand that medical examiners are not police officers. We have to maintain neutrality, and it is important that we ask questions. Either the medical examiner or the investigator will ask questions directly of the family in an effort to gather data about the decedent. The medical examiner's office usually bears the responsibility of notifying the family that a death has occurred. We try to bridge the gap between law enforcement, hospital, or private physicians, and the family. Often, what we do at the scene will assist law enforcement but we do not take their place. It remains important that families feel comfortable talking with the medical examiner's staff.

Only on rare occasions will I perform a postmortem examination with no information. In situations like this I perform the autopsy in order to gather information about the deceased.

The uniqueness of the human body and the knowledge of how cruel humans can be to one another is what motivates me to find out as much as possible about the deceased. Just as you have to open a book and read it to find out what it is about, the same approach is applied to finding out about a person's death. There is a story to be told in each and every case.

Science, Sympathy, And Sense

My ability to examine a dead human body and maintain respect for the deceased person as well as compassion for his grieving loved ones, combined with knowledge of the law and human anatomy is my God-given talent. My abilities are unique. My religious faith has brought me quite a long way. I do not mean to sound cliché or to plagiarize our beautiful Negro spirituals but that is how I feel. There is a scientific side to me that is compatible with my spiritual side. This is what allows me to look at everyone who comes to my attention and focus on that deceased person's individual needs for that particular time. Most forensic pathologists do not have the same approach to death as I do. I learned through my mentor, Joseph Davis, M.D., that medical examiners do, indeed, speak for the dead. We, as the forensic pathologists, are to tell the dead man's story. I have been taught through my apprenticeship and experience that if you look carefully with an open mind and a wide eye, the story is there. The body, as well as the complete investigation of death, will tell the story. It will be there if you care to find it. I care enough to find it.

I teach my students and staff that we cannot perform autopsies in a vacuum. We need knowledge of what transpired at death. That knowledge should include the health history and personal habits of the deceased. We, as the examiners, should strive to think outside of the box when reconstructing the death scene. We are formulating our opinions of what we think happened based upon logical thought, valid information, thorough investigation, and what exists within the realm of medical probability. For me, every time and every situation, I have not lost sight of the individuality of the dead person before me. Whether it is the body of an unborn fetus or an elderly person who has lived far into their twilight years, there is a story to be told. I must listen with my eyes, ears, hands, and all of my collective senses.

There are many ways that I look at death. One is to consider it as a blessing to those who are racked with pain and need peace, as well as to be welcomed by those who have lived long, full, active lives. To those in emotional pain, it may be a comfort. Studying death is one of the best ways to help others live longer, healthier lives. Death must be recognized and accepted as inevitable to humans. It should be considered part of the cycle of life. It remains the great unknown and uncertain finality and, therefore, frightening to many.

There are different categories of death that medical examiners use for the purpose of collecting vital statistics. Individuals who make decisions about our society use this statistical data. This is the reason that death and birth certificates are completed. A documented death is a vital record and important to the health of a community. The death certificate is a recording of the facts of death and is used to compile information about the population and to plan for the public health of a community.

Being a medical examiner can be quite a risky profession. You are going to be forever the bearer of bad news. You must stand on principles, ethics, and law. Many individuals are not going to understand why you do what you do and they often do not want to hear what you have to say, regarding death. The medical examiner, by virtue of his profession, is to be a neutral party who records the facts. He finds himself in numerous controversies or political situations. The medical examiner should be willing to assist all parties involved with death investigation. We must keep in mind that while we work with everyone as much as we can, we work for no one except the greater good of the public, which we serve.

There are laws that define what deaths medical examiners investigate and why. These laws vary region to region, according to the structure and type of government. They are the basis for a medical examiner to complete his work without fear of retribution because he has made an unpopular decision. Under ideal conditions the medical examiner should have no fear; however, we live in the real world. The medical examiner must possess a strong character to withstand the criticism and

downright meanness of some people when they do
not get their way. Many times the death
investigation process becomes ugly, because of
concerns over money or division of assets. One
thing I have affirmed time and time again as a
forensic pathologist is that while it is nice to have
money and material possessions, they do not change
your status in death. You cannot get more real than
this!

Despite the knowledge that I am a medical
examiner, who boldly states that I remain neutral, I
continue to receive calls from well-meaning
individuals in the community who consider
themselves affluent or politically inclined. They
may ask me if I will perform one case or another in
front of others because the decedent was a very
important person or from a wealthy family. I have
to remind these callers that in my office we treat

everybody like they were famous. This is the patient's last stop. I refuse to allow the poor, downtrodden, or homeless to be looked down upon in my office. No matter who the deceased person was, when he died he was human and he deserves dignity. Everybody was loved for a little while or, hopefully, created in love, and deserves the compassion that everybody wants and everybody needs at death. As a matter of fact, we have a VIP room in the Houston facility. It is called the very important person room because that is where examinations are performed on decomposed bodies. This designation is another reminder that no matter what your station in life, should the situation exist where a dead individual is not found in a reasonable amount of time, the body will undergo decomposition. It is another demonstration that death is the greatest equalizer of all individuals.

To be a doctor of the dead is to understand that you have to give a lot of yourself on a regular basis to the families who need you. A medial examiner must be able to renew this energy often. If you cannot let go of what you encounter in the workplace then the job will eventually extract a great emotional and physical toll. A long-lived medical examiner must develop a sense of balance and a way to separate his personal life from the cases with which he is involved. Those who cannot accomplish this personal goal often fail to reach a level of comfort with their work. I am blessed to have recognized my strength in this area many years ago.

The main responsibilities that I have as a medical examiner are to determine the cause and manner of death for individuals or groups of people. Cause and manner are often confused by clinical physicians as well as the general public. The cause

of death is what disease or injury has developed that

is incompatible with the continuation of life such as

a severe heart attack, multiple gunshot wounds,

malnutrition, or blunt trauma. The cause explains

the process by which life ends. How those diseases

or injuries occurred is the opinion that the medical

examiner renders as the manner of death. In other

words, because death is a constant, something has to

occur at the end to signal it. What happens to the

human body is the cause of death.

There are five common manners of death

that are used across the country: natural, homicide,

accident, suicide, and undetermined.

An undetermined category is used when we

have exhausted all possibilities of determining how

or why a person has died. Probably about three to

five percent of cases nationwide each year yield

undetermined manners of death. There is no statute

of limitation in forensic medicine. Old cases may

always be reinvestigated with valid and sufficient

information. This is the same basis for careful

scrutiny of DNA-involved cases. There may be new

ways to find answers to old questions.

One of the broadest categories in manner of

death and the one most commonly seen secondary

to natural disease is the accident. Accidental deaths

involve a wide variety of cases that range from

individuals who died in a hospital while undergoing

a surgical procedure to those who have died in

transportation accidents. This category includes the

number one cause of accidental deaths, motor

vehicle accidents. The opinion of accident is

determined after a complete investigation reveals

that a person, through no direct action of his own,

has died. To physicians, some accidental deaths

appear to have been avoidable but we realize that human nature has developed in such a way to assume that certain things will not occur, such as the possibility of being struck by lightning while playing golf in a thunderstorm.

There are some aspects of making an accidental death ruling that are somewhat disconcerting to the general public. These are the deaths of individuals who through their own unhealthy habits become addicted to certain elements, particularly drugs, whether they be prescription, illegal, or alcohol.

Alcohol use is included in the categories of natural as well as accidental deaths. This is due to the well-known, long-term side effects that alcohol has on the internal organs like cirrhosis or gastrointestinal bleeding. When the death occurs suddenly and there is no evidence of habitual drug use, it is called an accident, which is not an easy ruling to make. There are times when a family may ask why a drug-related death was not ruled an accident. This ruling occurs when the chronic use of drugs leads to the development of natural disease such as malnutrition, infections, organ failure, or cancer.

Manner of death can be a difficult ruling to make if an individual was taking a number of pills. The ruling is often made based on whether the drug was taken on one occasion leading to death or over an extended period. Often an investigation will reveal a chronic habit of abusing prescription drugs by a patient. There are other occasions when a thorough investigation reveals the individual did not have a clear understanding of the directions under which to take the drugs or there was a language barrier to understanding. The facts are that each case must be dealt with on an individual basis. The medical examiner must remain objective throughout the investigation in order to make an unbiased judgment on how a person's death occurred. Personally, I try to give the individual the benefit of doubt when drugs are involved. I realize that physical and emotional addictions are very strong motivators and the person cannot help himself. When investigating these type of cases, I may make the opinion of an accident where there appears to have been recreational use or a strong addiction.

There are other cases where the amount of drug is not elevated in the decedent's system, however, the person develops toxic effects as an individual reaction. Those cases may be given an accidental death ruling as well.

Homicides occur when someone has caused the death of another. This ruling is often straightforward when we are talking about stab wounds, gunshot wounds, or even strangulations. There are a number of cases investigated where the manner of death is not so clear cut. Frequently, these deaths involve investigation of very young children or the elderly. When the two extremes of life are examined, we have a lot of similarities. Many times the issue of neglect will arise when investigating the death of an infant or senior citizen. That neglect may comprise the lack of custodial care, withholding of food, and proper medical attention. The investigation of homicide-neglect cases may involve the evaluation of the ability of a new mother to care for her child, as well as the ability of an adult child to care for an aged parent who has become childlike and is in need of constant supervision. These opinions are based upon all available information and not just the physical appearance of the decedent's body. There are conditions that must be considered that produce lesions that mimic injuries or illness, and may be the result of physical or emotional problems. Making an opinion of homicide can be accomplished after a complete postmortem examination, complete police investigation, and laboratory tests are performed. It is not an opinion to be made lightly as there is a responsibility to ensure that the criminal justice system is supported through fact and documentation.

Opinions made by medical examiners as to how and why people die are often difficult and time-consuming. It is sad and offensive that the media continues to portray medical examiners as hardened, ill-mannered, quick-to- judge characters on television and in movies. There must be an understanding that death investigation takes time and good old-fashioned investigation. Because we live in a "now" generation, there is a tendency to expect the pathologist to rush into making opinions and not consider all the facts.

There are questions to be answered not only to the family but also to the treating physician. The most frequent question received from the private physician is why did a patient die? Not only is that a question, it is often a statement, "My patient should not have died." This statement is often made involving individuals who have died with evidence of chronic, debilitating, and aggressive diseases such as a brain injury or cancer. There are times when the family and the treating physician challenge the need to perform an autopsy when there is not a clear-cut cause of death or there may be contradicting causes of death. In certain cases there may be questions raised as to who died, where, and how. Often the family will ask why an autopsy is needed, especially if the cause of death is known. Investigators know what appears to be the cause, such as a traffic accident. Yes, the individual has wrecked his car, and that may be why he has died. At a swimming pool, the body was found in the water, and that could be why the person died. But things are not always what they seem. I want to know why the death occurred because it may help somebody else live a longer, more productive life.

Let's discuss the drowning victim. Why did he drown? Was it because he could not swim? Did he drown because he was under the influence of drugs or alcohol? Did he drown because he received an electrical shock from a faulty light in the swimming pool? Did he drown because he was hit on the head first and then thrown into the water? Did he drown because he had a seizure? These questions can often be answered upon completion of a thorough postmortem examination of the person, his social and medical background, and his circumstances of death.

Having performed the complete autopsy we are able to answer questions that may be posed by other parties, including insurance companies.

In addition, the mechanism of death, or the abnormal bodily functions that are incompatible to life, should be explained. Even though a person dies because he was shot, it is what the bullet did that is important to understand. Bullets by themselves create holes, but that is not why a person dies. The wounds usually create openings in blood vessels and organs, which allow blood to escape. Blood belongs inside of the vessels (vascular tree). When it leaves the vascular tree, the internal organs are then starved for oxygen and they have no source of energy. This is the ultimate result of a gunshot wound, as well as a drowning.

A person who drowns is unable to breathe because water adds an extra layer to the respiratory tissue and oxygen cannot be exchanged. So it is the same mechanism in both a gunshot wound and a drowning that the body tissue becomes starved for oxygen, particularly the central nervous system. These are extreme causes of death with the same ultimate consequences. The ability to explain the mechanism of death comes from basic knowledge and understanding of physiology and how the human body functions.

The medical examiner must have a good background in anatomy and physiology because we must recognize and document abnormal bodily function. The mechanism of death can be explained by the medical examiner to the jury and to families, as well as the treating physician. The medical examiner should be able to explain what happened in basic language in order to bridge the medical and legal aspects of a death investigation and allow the family to understand what happened to a loved one. This is why the forensic pathologist must understand the basics of biology, chemistry, and physics. We build upon this foundation with layers of anatomy and applications to the physical diagnosis of patients. Having applied all of this scientific background and medical knowledge we can then establish the cause, manner, and mechanism of death. Our documentation process is written in medical jargon to enable us to communicate with other physicians. We must, however, always remember that the reader of most of our reports does not have a medical background and we must keep the language simple to allow for greater understanding.

Natural deaths form the bulk of caseloads for most medical examiners. If you only pay attention to media highlights you would think the reverse were true. Most individuals die from natural causes. The medical examiner is often required to investigate deaths that occur at home or where the person was not under a doctor's care. Individuals who die within twenty-four hours of having been admitted to a hospital are often reported to the medical examiner and may be investigated. Those who expire in law enforcement custody may die from natural death. The homeless who have no medical history often die in public spaces. Many of the workplace deaths that we investigate involve people who die as a result of cancer, infection, or cardiovascular disease. By investigating natural deaths, medical examiners are able to give some comfort to families, inform the clinical physician, and add to the body of medical knowledge.

Forensic pathologists or medical examiners hold such a unique and privileged position within the medical community. The medical examiner must apply all of the skills necessary to do a scientific investigation, a medical evaluation, and communication of what was found. It is a privilege to investigate death. It can also be a daunting experience. The doctor must be well trained with a strong foundation, not only in medical education. He must have coping skills and a strong desire to do what is right. Without all of these variables the medical examiner would not be able to do his or her job. After all, if we don't have an open mind, like blank pages in a book, the decedent's story could never be written.

No-Win Situation

Deaths that occur when an individual is in the custodial care of others are classified as custody deaths. These cases include people who are in government-run nursing homes, orphanages, prisons, mental healthcare institutions and deaths that occur while being apprehended by law enforcement officers.

Police-custody deaths often result in civil unrest and many tense situations in urban areas. The most provocative cases are those where there has been public observance of police takedown procedures resulting in a potential suspect being injured or dying while engaging in a struggle. The videotaped beating of Rodney King by the Los Angeles police officers has become a flagship example of police brutality of all who witnessed this incident vicariously through the repetitive media coverage. Cases of alleged police brutality or misconduct have occurred in several major cities in recent years resulting in intense media coverage and civil disobedience. Other lesser known cases involve inmates who have died while in law enforcement custody in local jails or prisons. Often these deaths are unwitnessed and investigated long after the fatalities have taken place, if they are investigated at all. The abundant and mysterious jailhouse suicides in the mid-1990's that occurred in Mississippi are a prototype of this kind of questionable death.

I have had extensive experience in custody deaths, having served as a military officer and investigating deaths in federal prisons and serving as chief medical examiner in both Washington, D.C., and Houston, Texas. At the onset of a death-in-custody investigation, a well-trained medical examiner should expect questions from several areas such as family, police, political leaders, media, civil rights organizations, and the criminal justice system itself. First of all, you have a family who needs to understand how and why their loved one died. Second, you have the media who will be questioning how and why the individual died, particularly, when it is a slow news period. Third, you will have law enforcement that will need to understand why the death occurred. Also, there will be an entire community with citizens asking why and how the person died. Finally, you may encounter racially polarizing conditions. These are often volatile and may pit civilians against the police.

As a medical examiner and neutral investigator, my first obligation is to examine the body as fully as I would any other individual who has died. My other obligation is to realize that my work will be carefully scrutinized and there will be many individuals and groups who will have questions that may be answered through my report. I have to understand that the case needs to be done thoroughly and as rapidly as possible. I know from my experience and training that the medical examiner must maintain neutrality, be open-minded, and make himself available for questions that are going to continue throughout the investigation process.

The medical examiner must be of strong moral character and possess great intestinal fortitude to be able to withstand the political pressure that accompanies such volatile cases. It is not unusual for some party to attempt to persuade the forensic pathologist to place a certain spin on the autopsy findings. Often the community interest is fueled by the constant media replays when some police interaction results in an unexpected death. These are always highly emotional events and not the time for the medical examiner to lose his composure, but to maintain control over the situation. I have found that being honest, direct, and thorough with attention to all details has been the best relief for these very tense situations.

I have been involved in investigations of all ethnic groups who have died while in police custody and have found the ability to maintain a neutral stance to be important in all arenas. I believe that if you adhere to these guidelines you will be able to continue to serve the public. Of note is the reality that there are just not enough minority representatives involved in forensic medicine. The majority of fatalities where in-custody deaths occur appear to involve minority males, not surprisingly,

African-American first, and Hispanic men second. Seldom is there an occasion where an Asian male has been killed in police custody but it can happen. Last, but not least, is the consideration that white males are also killed in police custody, but when the percent of the population is counted the numbers are far lower than those in the minority populations.

When you consider all of the ethnic groups put together, there is a higher percentage of black males killed in police custody. Thus, there are sayings in the African-American community, "Living while black" or "Driving while black." From my personal experience as a black female, I can speak with authority when I say that one of a black person's nightmares is having a confrontation with police. I think that we as a country must look at our history closely to understand the fear and intimidation that a black person would have in a confrontation with law enforcement. Historically, police officers have been used to uphold the Jim Crow laws, such as using firearms, water hoses, or vicious animals against black people to enforce segregation laws. Law enforcement was used to prevent physical access by people of color in public places. There have been too many cases where black men have been killed in police custody followed by the eruption of violence and creating mob behavior, as has occurred in cities such as Miami, New York, Philadelphia, and Cincinnati. I think that we can all agree that you can change the law as was done with the passage of the Civil Rights Bill in the 1960s, however, you cannot change mind-sets with just legislation.

Our society has allowed negative and incorrect perceptions of black people to continue where those affecting other ethnic groups have diminished over time. I point again to the continuous bombardment through the media including written, audio, and visual forms when it comes to black stereotypes or mischaracterization. You cannot help but understand why the misperceptions and stereotypes that a person has grown up with are carried over into his social encounters. This has happened too much and has gone on far too long for some people to engage in healthy interactions. I can appreciate the hesitation, suspicion, and fear that the black male may have upon encountering police.

You have just to look back into African-Americans' history of being victims of lynching and racist antisocial groups, and even this country's laws which have not been changed enough for complete social acceptance of the person of color. This country has never apologized for slavery and has taken baby steps when it comes to erasing all the harm that slavery did to African-Americans. We must recognize that there is a level of stress that is an undercurrent in the black community and will probably always be there until we come to grips and accept the fact that people of color have not been treated fairly in this country. I think today that young African-American males, in particular, are tired, feel continuously stressed, and do not see change coming around quickly enough in the new century as it concerns interracial interactions. I remain concerned that many young black males have developed a sense of hatred of law enforcement and may not hesitate to show it. As an African-American forensic pathologist it remains my duty to be neutral in order to determine what has happened to an individual based upon all available information. Despite the racial overtones of these investigations, I cannot abdicate this principle.

Very seldom is there a true recording of what transpired when a custody death has occurred and investigators must ask witnesses what they saw. The investigator may ask three to four people and will probably get three or four variations of the truth. It is important that the medical examiner put together or reconstruct the scene free of bias, in a manner that will allow the greater public to have confidence in what he is reporting, recording, and documenting about the victim's death. I know that it is easier to receive bad news when it comes from a person who appears to be sensitive to the needs of the community and appears to have an open mind to all possibilities. A medical examiner who is perceived as being honest receives more acceptance when bearing bad news.

When there has been a police in-custody death, it is a negative situation for all parties. On behalf of the police, I can understand the necessary use of force on occasion. Each case must be analyzed on its own merit. In my past thirty years of experience I have witnessed many people, for whatever reason, who do not respect law enforcement or societal laws. I still believe that there are more honest police officers than there are bad. As in every situation, to stereotype all police officers as being racist or out of control is just as wrong as believing the stereotypes about people of color. Many times my investigations have supported the premise that most police officers want to do their job to protect the greater society and do not want to shoot and kill. From strictly a fact basis, law-enforcement officers from time to time encounter individuals who reject their authority or are acting under the influence of alcohol or drugs and present a danger to themselves and the community.

At the same time, I have investigated cases where the officer has been too quick to shoot or use excessive force in apprehending a potential suspect or in taking care of an individual who had erratic behavior due to drugs or alcohol. In many situations the police officers have to make a judgment call. Who will shoot first? On one hand I can sympathize with the police officer who may feel threatened when encountering an individual who is belligerent or who seems fearless to use a weapon. What would you do if you were in a similar situation and when would you know if it was going to be the threat that becomes reality?

On the other hand, you have the average citizen who happens to be black or Hispanic, minding his own business, who is pulled over because he fits the general description of a suspect and ends up in a confrontation, or sometimes dead. The situation is always critical. It is always sad. There is rarely a winner. When all the dust has settled, someone has died and someone must be held accountable for the death. Whether it is a citizen or a police officer that is killed, it still remains a tragedy for our community. From my viewpoint there will always be two sets of victims, the perpetrator and his family and the victim's family. These people will be left to pick up the pieces and to question why.

As a black female physician it pains me when I examine the harsh numbers that show one of the greatest manners of death in the black community is homicide. Fifty percent of all homicide victims in this country are African-

American. Included in the homicide classification are in-custody deaths involving police interaction. I do not have any answers for the problems of racism in this country. I do feel that some of the civil unrest that occurs during the investigation of in-custody deaths would be ameliorated if there were more people of various ethnic backgrounds involved in the investigation of these deaths.

I know one thing for certain. We must start using equality with our children. We must act together as a country, as a group of people who are more closely related than we are different. Perhaps if we start early in educating our children that they are alike, there is no superiority and no reason to fear another individual because he is different, then, in time, these in-custody death rates will change.

Another sensitive area of death where I become involved in investigating are cases where a public safety officer has been killed. Unfortunately, I have been involved in too many of these cases. When a police officer is killed in the line of duty the entire law-enforcement community comes together, for the most part, arm in arm, hand in hand, whether the officer was black, tan, red, yellow, or white. The police come together in a way that must be respected in support of their fallen comrade or comrades. I have found when dealing with fallen police officers, the situation becomes quite tense. In similar fashion to in-custody death, the medical examiner is going to experience cases where there will be a lot of questions ranging from the quality of the police uniforms and equipment down to the appropriate length of police training. Elected officials will have questions from their constituents and the media will ask questions and put their interpretation of the crime scene onto the airwaves

and print. There may be a brief period where the
community comes together in mourning and asks
why, as was the case with the events of September
11, and any time a local police officer dies in the
line of duty.

I frequently attend the scene when a law-
enforcement officer has been killed in the line of
duty. I recognize in many cases that police are
constantly interacting with individuals who do not
have the same regard for our society's laws. In
many ways I can understand the policeman's level
of stress. Unfortunately, the most common site of
fatal wounding in the law enforcement officer is the
head. It is somewhat ironic that police officers are
trained to shoot in the body or the extremities while
more of our civilians are willing to shoot an officer
in the head. Deaths of public-safety officers
demand immediate attention and present challenges

to every community. I must exercise the same concern and investigative techniques to fulfill my role as a neutral death investigator. The sad commentary is that the community rarely recognizes our public safety officers in life, either by fair pay grade or everyday courtesy. I find it appalling that law enforcement officers of all colors and ethnic groups, who, on a daily basis, put their lives on the line, are in the end paid some of the lowest salaries in the community. Public safety officers rank next to the way we treat teachers who educate our children. We seldom thank the police officer for doing a good job, and yet when we are in trouble officers are the first people we call on. Local law enforcement agencies have begun community policing. Hopefully, one day this involvement with the community will again elevate law enforcement officials to the respectful ranks that they deserve.

Whether a civilian is killed by a police officer or a police officer is killed by a civilian, the outcome is the same. A no-win situation results in increased community tension.

Prayer, Faith, and Healing

The medical community could benefit from learning that a sense of spirituality in a physician is a good thing. There is a lot of documentation in current periodicals indicating that a physician who is prayerful and willing to acknowledge the patient's faith often has a happier, more emotionally stable patient, a higher success rate with procedures, and a shorter period of morbidity (illness). The same goes for the patient's family or loved ones who have to deal with the death. It is a good thing for a physician to have professional distance, but it is another to engage the individual on a spiritual level. I have observed that when there is no will to live or there is no faith in what the doctor can do, then a patient may have a more difficult time recovering from his illness or even surviving. I am a great believer in the combination of faith and prayer to assist the patient in healing. I do not hesitate to let a family know that I have Christian values and I respect faiths of all kinds.

I have found that when families are reluctant to have postmortem procedures performed it is helpful to ask if they will allow their religious leader to talk with me or even to observe the postmortem examination. Many times if we explain our procedures to a family's religious leader the family will have more acceptance of what has to be done under the law. By joining on their spiritual level we are able to allay many fears that their loved one's body will be harmed or in some way disrespected. I have had many religious leaders join me in the morgue.

There are several procedures that I use to help the family feel comfortable and to let them know that what I am doing is not only upholding the law, but will be of benefit to them. It is important that communication is not overlooked in the practice of good medicine and the delivery of care. Not only does my religious faith allow me to place each and every decedent on the same level as my own family, but it allows me to open my heart to the emotional pain that surviving family and friends are experiencing. I am not trying to convert anyone to my faith but I allow them in their own way to call upon their spiritual reserves. I have had many families of different faiths and socioeconomic levels as well as ethnic backgrounds come in for a conference.

Oftentimes these individuals are tense and angry when they enter the room. These same people will exit with hugs while voicing well wishes. The common denominator has always been, "Thank you for listening to me; thank you for caring." I credit this change with my spirituality and ability to empathize with all of these individuals at their moment of need. It is important that I am sincere about wanting them to understand what I do to their loved ones' body. I will admit that I am one of those hugging doctors, if that is what it takes, because the family and I can connect on that level. Sometimes, a grieving person needs a hug. You can talk all of the medical jargon you want but if you break down your words with sincerity and with a sense of loss for the family, you are reaching across the ocean to touch land. These are not tricks. It is a way of recognizing that, as a physician, you must use the calmness that spirituality gives you to handle a difficult situation. I consistently tell the public that if you are a praying person and your doctor is not a prayerful doctor, then you need to find a new doctor. Faith and healing go hand in hand.

There is such a sharp divide between life and death on the medical level that there is no question as to why this subject is a problem in the hospital. The morgue is completely separated from patient care areas and I am not advocating that this change, but when death occurs in a hospital setting there is complete separation between the treating physician and the pathologist in the hospital. Very seldom do pathologists have interaction with other physicians, who often have no idea of what families go through after death occurs. Most physicians do not interact with their patients' family to know the difficulty that the family experiences in planning a funeral after a sudden, unexpected death; choosing a cemetery; gathering their loved ones' belongings from hospital storage, or finding out what the

medical examiner's procedures will be. Most
hospital physicians cannot explain what the medical
examiner is going to do or why.

When families have questions about
postmortem procedures, that is the time to perhaps
make use of the hospital chaplain or other
individuals who are trained to be calm and give
spiritual guidance when death has occurred. There
should be more interaction with chaplains,
ministers, and other spiritual people of various
faiths and denominations with healthcare providers.
These individuals should be exposed to the medical
student, as well as, the mature physician. I feel if
these services were made available to more patients
there would be more compliancy with prescription
medications, acceptance of medical diagnoses, and
an increase in the ability to handle harsh diagnoses.
It is my experience that physicians who make

known their beliefs in a higher power while dealing with patients who also believe are more successful. In my world there can be no compromise between prayer, faith and healing. While I do not handle the living patient in a sense, I must help their survivors heal. A lot of our healing comes by faith and prayer. In the world of death these cannot be separate issues.

Aftercare

I believe the main reason I have been successful in maintaining my examination skills is that I have never forgotten the "need to know" by the family, first and foremost. I have never lost the feeling that I would like to have my own deceased loved ones treated in the same way that I treat others when I am performing an autopsy. I feel that once you lose that attachment, that concern, then you tend to become careless or harsh in your approach to that dead body. We, as medical examiners, have got to care, no matter how heavy the load. I have always been serious about the Hippocratic Oath that I took upon graduation from medical school. When I no longer have the ability to feel or empathize, then I need to find another occupation. I am grateful for my gift and I will always be energized by my ability to help others.

No matter how tired I am when I start out in the morning or when the day is done, I have found some answers somewhere to help someone. When I can explain to a family how and why their loved one has died, I feel good. Many times families do not like what I have to tell them but at least they do not feel left out of the loop. Family, friends, and survivors should not feel victimized by the bureaucracy of a government death investigation system.

Often, just by following the directions to receive an autopsy report, families and friends will not receive the answers that they need. There is no reason for them to feel aggravated when they are already dealing with the loss of life. Forensic pathologists have to remember when we are dealing with an angry, belligerent, or even physically threatening family member that he is also dealing with bigger issues. A sudden change has occurred whether the person has lost a lifetime partner, a child, a parent, or whomever, his life will never be the same.

Medical examiners have to realize that families come to us out of concern and fear. When they are informed that their loved one has died they have not been prepared for that moment. Many of them are simply not in their right state of mind. They exist in a very volatile and fragile emotional state and that is when they are most apt to say unkind words, curse you, and threaten you verbally or with physical harm. It takes a strong sense of patience to overlook the reactions because the individuals are grieving. There is nothing that says that any two people must go through grief in the same manner. No matter how it feels to one person, until the worst scenario happens to you, it is nearly impossible to imagine an individual's reaction to grief.

There is a need for postmortem aftercare. I consider this counseling and education of family and friends who have lost a loved one and need answers to many questions. Families should feel comfortable knowing they can call upon the medical examiner to sit down and talk to them face-to-face to help them understand. Each and every family should be treated in the same respectful way. As I have stated before, medical examiners are in no position to condemn. This is the time to help a grieving person. This is where, in many cases, special training is needed. The medical examiner should posses good communication skills and have a forgiving nature because he is going to be dealing with emotionally charged individuals. We are the bearers of bad news, and the families often do not

want to hear what we have to say. There are times
when we may have to tell a wife that her deceased
husband had numerous sexually transmitted
diseases and was HIV-positive. We must be
prepared for the reaction that the survivors may
have.

I often conduct my family counseling
sessions in a serene quiet area. I may ask family
members to bring along their religious leader for
support, or their family physician, or a friend for
stability. Many times, if it is a large family, I will
meet with two members at a time to reduce the
possible hysteria that may ensue when the bad news
is broken. There are times when the surviving
people apologize to me for crying. I always say to
them, "Everyone has his own way of grieving.
Whether you cry or not is your individual reaction."
For those who do not cry, it does not mean you did

not feel anything for the person who is dead. I encourage families to take their time to talk about what has happened with someone whom they trust. I have had families contact me days, months, or even years after a loved one's death. I had one family contact me thirty years after a death had occurred. Of course I had not performed the postmortem examination but they asked me for help and I did everything that I could because they were ready to deal with the issue. Sometimes aftercare means that people are ready to discuss a person's death.

Many families have questions concerning procedures that are in place in the medical examiners office. The most common question our office receives is, "When will we have an answer about the cause of death?" This is a very difficult question because it depends on the circumstances of death. What I try to tell families is to let my department do an assessment, then make them aware of the steps that have to be taken in order to resolve some issues and document the death, as well as determine the cause and manner. I give them my word that I will contact them at least every two weeks with progress and let them know the procedures that are going to have to be taken in their particular loved one's case. I then remind the family that all cases are different and must be looked at as individual examinations. When families have this type of response, at least they know their questions have been given some consideration and they have become part of the system instead of being completely on the outside wondering what is going on.

There are other questions that are frequently raised by family and friends. One is, when will a loved one's body be released? In the office that I currently serve, bodies that are received for examination are usually ready for release to the funeral home within twenty-four to forty-eight hours. So long as the identification is made and the examination has been performed, that body may be released to the funeral home of the family's choice. Usually bodies are retained longer if there is an unusual or complex homicide case, extensive decomposition, or some severe injury or special examinations that require an outside related forensic expert to consult on the case. The least I can do is be honest with the person asking the questions and give him a framework of the examination and what it is going to take to complete the forensic work and develop an opinion as to the cause and manner of death.

Another question asked is where can the family or friends pick up the deceased's personal effects? That answer also depends on the situation and circumstances of death. If the individual has been brought in from an accident scene or a workplace or public space, then those personal effects usually arrive with the body. If an individual was taken to a medical facility for treatment prior to his demise, then his belongings have usually been removed for examination and are retained by the hospital or collected by law enforcement. Again, it depends on what happened. There are times when the personal effects are retained as evidence, if it is felt they are related to the disease or injury that caused a person's death. Many times clothing has been destroyed by the emergency medical team trying to save the victim's life.

Part of aftercare involves notifying the family when death has occurred and explaining the unnatural appearance of their loved one.

Sometimes grieving people contact me because they are searching for a missing loved one. I urge them to never give up hope and to work with their local law enforcement and missing persons bureau. It is possible for medical examiners and law enforcement agencies to keep in contact via computer and missing person bulletins. It is not unusual that a person can leave his local area and be across the country in a matter of days. All medical examiner offices receive bodies that are unidentified. Many of these individuals are identified within thirty-six hours of being at the medical examiner's office because all unknown decedents are fingerprinted. There are many cases, however, where the decedent remains a John or

Jane Doe. These unidentified bodies are often people who have left home and no one thought to look for them or even considered that they had died. I wonder about the young teens who arrive in major cities daily looking for a better, or more exciting life and end up as victims of violent crimes. It is sad when a young person is not searched for. It is sad when an older person is not looked for. I have been involved in cases where a senior citizen's body would be brought into the office and it would be six weeks before their family members, living in the same town, realized the person had died. It goes to show that there is a constant need for communication within our nuclear families.

Another question that I am asked by families, health professionals and visitors to the medical examiner office is, "How do you cope with the examination of a decomposed body?" I always have a very simple answer: "Those decomposed human remains are simply the results of Mother Nature working on our flesh. Mother Nature can do in a few days what we use thousands of chemicals to retard. There is a distinct odor and appearance to a decomposed body. But, no matter the condition of those human remains, they represent a person who was once alive. There is no way to determine whether our lives will end with our bodies being found immediately or in days, weeks, or months. Some forensic investigators find the decomposed body unpleasant to work on. I, on the other hand, find the casework challenging, and often rewarding. If a careful examination is performed on that decomposed body, including full X-rays and scene investigation, a lot of information may be gained. Forensic scientists can often reunite the remains of that human being with his family or arrive at a conclusion as to how and why the person died."

The media portrayal of medical examiner offices frequently detracts from the serious responsibilities of the medical examiner. I have viewed many television movies and primetime shows where a family must come in to identify a deceased relative. The scene is always the same. The emotionally distraught family member is brought in by a gruff detective, taken into the morgue where a steel drawer is pulled open and a sheet abruptly removed showing the grotesque face and body of that person's loved one. Aside from the dramatic flare for television, I always feel terrible for the image left with a grieving person. First of all, most individuals fear the dead. Many people fear being where dead bodies are. Most will have the worst nightmares and harsh feelings of having been shown their loved one's body in such a crude way.

Death notification and identification is the time for gentleness. I do not understand why television shows like that drawer effect but I wish Hollywood producers would find a more humane way to identify bodies. This adds to the stereotype of medical examiner's office and morgues being more like *Frankenstein* movies. What normally transpires in the medical examiner's office is that the family is brought into the facility and usually shown a Polaroid photograph of their presumed relative. The photograph may show the face or perhaps an usual scar or tattoo that the family could recognize and identify. If the photograph is not suitable, then the family is taken into a quiet room where the body can be viewed through a plate-glass wall. In this way the family does not have to go into the morgue and they are able to look at their loved one's body without any fear of touching it or risking contamination of evidence.

There are other stereotypes that lead to misperceptions of the public when they come to the morgue to identify a loved one. Movies and television programs often show an individual walking into the morgue, being startled by the body in the drawer, and saying, "Yes, that's him." That is not quite the way it happens when we have a murder victim. The body of a homicide victim must be identified under legal circumstances, which include fingerprint comparison, dental examination, or DNA. It is not enough just to have visual identification by a family member. I often explain to families that after the person they knew and loved has died those characteristics that we recognize are no longer present. We recognize people by their smile, the way their eyes flicker, or even the muscular tension of their facial expressions. These features are gone at death.

We also live in a time and place where people can alter their identities by changing clothes, hair color, or even by plastic surgery. We must be aware of these conditions. Currently, forensic investigators not only use these legal identifying techniques but also include X-rays that can demonstrate previous surgical sites, arthritic changes in the skeletal system, and the individual characteristics of our nasal sinuses.

The final question that I receive from a multitude of survivors is. "How do you cope with dealing with the dead?" This question brings this book and discussion full circle. How I deal with the dead is the gift I believe God gave to me. It is not a matter of me dealing with the dead, it is the responsibility that I have to care for them. I consider myself the last healthcare professional to examine the deceased's body. There is an old joke in medical circles that says, "Surgeons do everything but know nothing, internists know everything but do nothing, and pathologists know everything and do everything, but it is too late." I like to feel that I know enough to help somebody. I am going to do enough to get answers. And I am going to do it in a way that tells the dead person's story so that his death is not in vain and the information gained from examining him will help somebody else.

I hope that this book has been a blessing to someone dealing with the pain of grief. If it does not answer all of your questions, perhaps it gives you a starting point from which to ask them. For those who are grieving, I send my prayers, and I wish comfort in your long days. Remember to take your sorrow one day at a time. For those who need answers that were not entertained in this book, I pray you will find the strength to ask them. To all reading, God bless. Be well.

Contact Information

Please send your questions or requests to:

Joye M. Carter, M.D.

P.O. Box 2096

Kensington, MD 208911-2096

Website: www.joyemcarter.com

Email: joyemcartermd@aol.com or

biblicaldogs@aol.com